The
National Exp
Handboo

British Bus Publishing

Body codes used in the Bus Handbook series:

Type:

A	Articulated vehicle
B	Bus, either single-deck or double-deck
BC	Interurban - high-back seated bus
C	Coach
M	Minibus with design capacity of 16 seats or less
N	Low-floor bus (*Niederflur*), either single-deck or double-deck
O	Open-top bus (CO = convertible; PO = partial open-top)

Seating capacity is then shown. For double-decks the upper deck quantity is followed by the lower deck.

Door position:-

C	Centre entrance/exit
D	Dual doorway.
F	Front entrance/exit
R	Rear entrance/exit (no distinction between doored and open)
T	Three or more access points

Equipment:-

L	Lift for wheelchair	TV	Training vehicle.
M	Mail compartment	RV	Used as tow bus or engineers vehicle.
T	Toilet	w	Vehicle is withdrawn and awaiting disposal.

e.g. - B32/28F is a double-deck bus with thirty-two seats upstairs, twenty-eight down and a front entrance/exit.
N43D is a low-floor bus with two or more doorways.

Re-registrations:-

Where a vehicle has gained new index marks the details are listed at the end of each fleet showing the current mark, followed in sequence by those previously carried starting with the original mark.

Regional books in the series:

The Scottish Bus Handbook
The Ireland & Islands Bus Handbook
The North East Bus Handbook
The Yorkshire Bus Handbook
The North West Bus Handbook
The East Midlands Bus Handbook
The West Midlands Bus Handbook
The Welsh Bus Handbook
The Eastern Bus Handbook
The London Bus Handbook
The South East Bus Handbook
The South West Bus Handbook

Annual books are produced for the major groups:

The Stagecoach Bus Handbook
The Go-Ahead Bus Handbook
The First Bus Handbook
The Arriva Bus Handbook
The National Express Handbook (bi-annual)
Most editions for earlier years are available direct from the publisher.

Associated series:

The Hong Kong Bus Handbook
The Malta Bus Handbook
The Leyland Lynx Handbook
The Model Bus Handbook
The Postbus Handbook
The Overall Advertisement Bus Handbook - Volume 1
The Toy & Model Bus Handbook - Volume 1 - Early Diecasts
The Fire Brigade Handbook (fleet list of each local authority fire brigade)
The Police Range Rover Handbook

Contents

The National Express Handbook

The National Express Handbook is part of The Bus Handbook series that details the fleets of selected bus and coach operators. These Bus Handbooks are published by *British Bus Publishing*. The current list is shown on page 2. This book lists the operators that operate services during the Summer 2004 timetable and details all the vehicles in National Express colours that are used on these services. Several of the seasonal routes use vehicles in operator's own colours and, as the vehicles may vary, only the route information is given. A summary of euroLines route from the UK or Eire is also included. An index of National Express and euroLines services is given at the back of the book along with an index of the contracted vehicles.

Quality photographs for inclusion in the series are welcome and a fee is payable. The publishers unfortunately cannot accept responsibility for any loss and request you show your name on each picture or slide.

To keep the fleet information up to date we recommend the Ian Allan publication, **Buses** published monthly, or for more detailed information, the PSV Circle monthly news sheets.

The writer and publisher would be glad to hear from readers should any information be available which corrects or enhances that given in this publication.

Series Editor: Bill Potter
Principal Editor for *The National Express Handbook:* **Bill Potter, Stuart Martin and David Donati.**

Acknowledgments:
We are grateful to National Express and euroLines management, Stephen Byrne, Mike Lambden, the PSV Circle and the operating companies for their assistance in the compilation of this book. The cover photograph is by Bill Potter in cooperation with National Express.

Earlier editions of the National Express Bus Handbook:
1st Edition - 2000 - ISBN 1-897990-56-1
2nd Edition - 2002 - ISBN 1-897990-58-8

ISBN 1 904875 04 1 (2004 Edition)
Published by *British Bus Publishing Ltd, 16 St Margaret's Drive*, Telford, TF1 3PH

Telephone: 01952 255669 - Facsimile 01952 222397 - www.britishbuspublishing.co.uk
© British Bus Publishing Ltd, September 2004

NATIONAL EXPRESS

National Express Ltd, 4 Vicarage Road, Edgbaston, Birmingham, B15 3ES

National Express is the market leader of scheduled coach services around the UK. Its now familiar red, white and blue coaches have been a traditional sight on the UK's roads for well over 30 years. But just when and where did this unique transport operation start?

The Early Days

Although stagecoaches were undoubtedly the forerunners of the present long-distance coach network, it was not until after the First World War and the introduction of motor buses that express coach services really came into their own.

In 1919, Elliott Bros., whose coaches carried the famous 'Royal Blue' fleet name, and who had actually run one of the earlier horse-drawn services, introduced a limited form of express coach service operating between Bournemouth and London.

However, Greyhound Motors of Bristol are generally acknowledged as being the first to introduce a daily, all year round, motorised express coach service in Britain. Their service, introduced in 1925, linked Bristol with London and expanded rapidly. Many other operators, able to see the commercial benefits of long distance travel, introduced similar services in the following months.

The first livery applied under the National Bus Company is seen on Duple-bodied Leyland Leopard OHE264X, seen at Victoria Coach Station which was also the site of the NBC Headquarters. *Tony Wilson*

The 1930 Road Traffic Act introduced a system of licensing that covered drivers, conductors and the routes that were operated. The introduction of the Act successfully brought order to a chaotic, rapidly growing, and somewhat haphazard industry. Intending bus and coach operators now found it much harder to introduce new services, with each application for a new or revised service requiring a lengthy application to the local government appointed Traffic Commissioner. This new system of licensing provided the stability for expansion and early co-operation amongst coach operators gave rise to the formation of the first networks of co-ordinated services.

These 'Pool' networks greatly increased travel opportunities for the rapidly growing number of coach passengers. Two of the most famous coaching 'Pools' were Associated Motorways, based at Cheltenham, and London Coastal Coaches, based at the new Victoria Coach Station. Opened in 1932, the new coach station replaced the original 'London' terminus in Lupus Street, which had opened in 1924.

Coaching develops

The decades following were good times for the coaching industry and the steady increase in the numbers of coach passengers peaked in the late 50's. In 1959 the opening of the first stretches of Britain's new motorway network brought new opportunities for coach operators such as Midland Red of Birmingham and Ribble of Preston with their 'Gay Hostess' double deck coaches. This was followed by a gradual decline in coach business the 1960s due to the increase in the number of private cars.

By the late sixties most bus companies, with the exception of municipal and small independent operators, had formed into two main groups, the state owned Tilling Group and the British Electric Traction Group (BET). In March 1968, the government brought both groups together under the Transport Holding Company.

The 1968 Transport Act brought about an integrated public passenger transport system across the country. One of the major provisions of the Act was the formation, on 28 November 1968, of the National Bus Company (NBC). NBC began operating on 1 January 1969 and, by 31 December 1969, NBC controlled 93 bus companies grouped into 44 operating units employing 81,000 staff and having a fleet of 21,000 vehicles. A new era of public transport had arrived.

Network Developments

From the beginning, the directors of what was the biggest road passenger transport operation in Europe began to bring together the coaching activities of each constituent operator. The reasons were obvious, each local company was pursuing its own policy of express coach service operation.

Inevitably this was leading to duplication of services and it was soon decided that a co-ordinated policy of express coach service planning would be of benefit to both the customer and the National Bus Company alike.

However regulation of services prevented any real network expansion or the provision of routes where there were mass markets.

The 'National' brand name was introduced during 1972 and the original 'all white' livery began to appear on coaches during 1973 as a first stage in offering customers a nationwide standard and a recognisable product. The winter of 1973/74 saw the publication of the first comprehensive coach timetable that included details of the entire 'National' network.

The new brand name 'National Express' first appeared on publicity material in 1974 and on vehicles during 1978. It was during this time that the 'EXTRA' computer reservations system was also brought into operation giving an improved service to both customers and booking agents by speeding up ticket issues.

In 1979, NBC commissioned a major programme of market research called 'Coachmap'. Every passenger on every journey was asked where, when and why he or she was travelling. The substantial amount of information obtained gave a much-needed insight into the travel requirements of both young and old but was never actually implemented as the 1980 Transport Act altered the whole of the network.

Deregulation and Expansion

The introduction, on 6 October, of the 1980 Transport Act, swept away 50 years of licensing restrictions and introduced competition on long distance coach routes.

National Express, and the main Scottish express coach operator, Scottish Citylink, faced new competition from a host of established bus and coach operators trying their hand at operating regular long distance coach services. It came as no surprise to National Express to discover that many of the 'new' operators seemed only to want to run coaches at the busiest times on the most popular routes. The future of the nationwide coach network, and of National Express itself, was in jeopardy.

Totally without subsidy, and by introducing new services and lower fares, National Express fought to win or perish in the ensuing war. Most of the new operators were unable to sustain continued viable operation and withdrew from operating their services within a matter of months. Even the co-operative venture mounted countrywide under the title 'British Coachways' failed to capture sufficient business.

The strengths of the nationwide, co-ordinated network operated by National Express became all too apparent and the publicity surrounding the 'coach war' gave a major boost to the long-term fortunes of National Express. Customers also benefited from these new services and lower fares and the skirmish gave National Express valuable experience that was to prove useful in the years to come. Most importantly National Express was free to provide coach services wherever it felt that there was a market.

In the late 1980s, National Express, Plaxtons and Volvo created a new purpose-built coach, the Expressliner, which was unveiled on 20 March 1989. The Expressliner, with a 'kneeling' suspension and many other features unique to National Express, brought a new standard of high quality coach travel across all routes, and today there are over 400 of its successors operating on routes across Britain. Seen in Aldgate a decade ago, H643UWR illustrates the model. *Tony Wilson*

On board catering

With skilful marketing and an eye for the needs of the customer, a handful of independent coach operators fared better than most. Both Trathens from the West Country and Cotters from Scotland (later to become Stagecoach) introduced up-market services operated by coaches carrying hostesses and refreshments and fitted with toilets.

Seeing the opportunities that such an operation would present on other services, National Express entered into an agreement with Trathens to co-operate in running the West Country services. This new concept of improved customer care and service quality was given the name 'Rapide' . The Rapide service introduced a hostess/steward service of light refreshments to each seat. The coaches used on the service were fitted with their own toilet/washroom, air suspension and reclining seats. The on-board facilities cut out the need for time consuming refreshment and toilet stops offering an instant saving, in journey times, of around 20%.

Public demand for the new Rapide services was initially high. It brought about the introduction of a new design of coach to cater for the increasing number of first-time customers who were now discovering the benefits of coach travel. However, the demand for this on-board catering was short-lived and seen to be declining in the late 1990s.

On-board surveys showed that an increasing number of customers were choosing to bring their own style of refreshments with them for their journey. This coupled with improvements to catering outlets at key coach and bus stations resulted in the gradual withdrawal of this facility, and by the start of the 2001 summer timetable it had been withdrawn from all National Express services However it still remains in place on some airport services as an additional benefit to the airport customer.

Annual passenger figures for the nationwide express coach network increased from 8.5 million in 1979 to around 15 million in 1986 as a direct result of post-deregulation competition. Today, the annual figure is around 16.5 million and is showing a small but steady annual growth. The main difference now is that the summer peaks that were experienced on some of the more popular services have now disappeared and coach services are now much busier · throughout the whole of the year.

'National Express' is Born

On 26 October 1986, following the introduction of the 1985 Transport Act there was deregulation within the industry to all local bus services. Although designed to increase competition between all bus and coach operators there was surprisingly little change in the long distance express coach market; it deregulated back in 1980.

However, of greater importance to National Express was the requirement that the National Bus Company should be sold into the Private Sector. The first subsidiary, National Holidays, was sold in July 1986; the last, London Country (North East) in April 1988.

National Express itself was the subject of a management buy-out, led by Clive Myers, on 17 March 1988. Between 1988 and 1991, National Express Holdings Ltd, the name of the company set up to buy National Express from the National Bus Company, acquired the established North Wales bus and coach operator, Crosville Wales, the Merseyside based coach operator Amberline, the ATL Holdings Group (which included the Carlton PSV vehicle dealership and the Yelloway Trathen bus and coach company mentioned earlier) and the express coach services of Stagecoach Holdings Ltd based in Perth.

It was during this period that National Express, Plaxtons and Volvo created a new purpose-built coach, the Expressliner, which was unveiled on 20 March 1989. The Expressliner, with a 'kneeling' suspension and many other features unique to National Express, brought a new standard of high quality coach travel across all routes, and today there are over 400 of its successors operating on routes across Britain.

Dunn-Line's ECZ9139 is one of the few Plaxton Excalibur coaches in National Express Livery. It is seen in Milton Keynes. *Dave Heath*

Scottish activity

The acquisition of the express coach services of the Stagecoach Holdings Group on 31 July 1989 came at the same time as the long-standing agreement with Scottish Citylink coaches on joint operation across the English/Scottish border came to an end.

To market the new Scottish network, 'Caledonian Express' was introduced as a new brand. The Caledonian Express offices were based at the old Stagecoach premises at Walnut Grove in Perth. Tied in to the main National Express network, Caledonian Express began to grow immediately. New double-decker coaches entered service on the prestige Rapide services linking London with Scotland and new marketing initiatives were introduced offering a high quality coach service to Scotland for the first time.

In 1993 National Express Group acquired Scottish Citylink. This acquisition enabled the Group to offer a truly 'national' coach network with services operating throughout England, Scotland and Wales. However, in August 1998, following the award in April of the franchise to operate ScotRail, Scotland's national railway, National Express Group disposed of Scottish Citylink to Metroline in a deal which left the operation intact but guaranteed the continuation of cross-border travel, using both companies' services, to enable customers to experience a seamless journey.

Flotation

Throughout its long and varied history, National Express has faced many changes. On 23 July 1991, a consortium made up of a number of city investment companies and the Drawlane Transport Group bought out National Express Holdings Ltd.

The chairman of the Drawlane Transport Group, Ray McEnhill, moved from that position and became the Chief Executive of the new company National Express Group Limited. Crosville Wales and Amberline were not included in the deal.

On 1 December 1992, National Express took another change of direction when Chief Executive Ray McEnhill and deputy chief executive Adam Mills led National Express Group onto the Stock Market through the London Stock Exchange at a share price of 165p.

The prospectus issued at the time of the flotation made the Group's new strategy for development clear. Its objectives were to refocus and improve the profitability of the core coach business, develop new products and services within its existing operations and acquire new businesses in the passenger transport market.

On 23 March 1993, National Express Group PLC sold its coach dealership, Carlton PSV Ltd leaving, as the main subsidiaries, National Express Ltd, Eurolines (UK) Ltd and Speedlink Airport Services Ltd.

Group Growth

The National Express Group's stated policy was to further expand the group by acquisitions within associated areas of the travel industry. This expansion took place not only in the UK but also within Europe and internationally.

During 1993 the group started these purchases with one of the first major acquisitions being the Amsterdam based company, Eurolines Nederland BV, which helped to strengthen the growing Eurolines network of European coach services. In the UK this was quickly followed with a successful bid for East Midlands Airport.

The press release at the time stated '...the acquisition of East Midlands Airport offers growth opportunities in a related area of business where National Express can apply its passenger handling and transport expertise.' Bids for other UK airports followed resulting in the purchase of Bournemouth International Airport.

The merger of National Express with West Midlands Travel (later to become Travel West Midlands), one of Europe's largest urban bus operations based in Birmingham, and the acquisition of Taybus Holdings, a Dundee based bus company, ensured that the group had interests within the UK bus industry.

The privatisation of the UK rail industry meant that the National Express Group expanded even further during 1996 with the acquisition of both the Gatwick Express and Midland MainLine franchises offering development for the group in yet another mode of public transport. Early in 1997 the Group acquired three more rail companies – North London Railways (soon to be renamed SilverLink), Central Trains and Scotrail making it one of the largest UK rail operators.

Overseas development during 1998/9 included the acquisition of a number of American School Bus operations including the Crabtree Harman Corporation, Robinson Bus Service and Durham Transportation which put NEG into the position of one of the top three US school bus operators, with over 1,750 vehicles operating daily. The Group later acquired a similar school bus operation in Canada during 2002.

Meanwhile on the other side of the world in Australia, the Group was also acquiring bus operations in Melbourne, Brisbane, Sydney and Perth, with additional rail/bus operations in Melbourne and the State of Victoria. National Express had become a truly global transport Group.

As a result of these developments, the National Express Group has now become a leading mass passenger transport services company – with over one billion passenger journeys being made on its range of services during 2002.

Investments

As a company, National Express has always been keen to make offer appropriate investments into the business. Over the years these have included developments in ticketing technology, coach design and a major coach station replacement programme.

It was during 1994 that the first purpose built coach station to be constructed in Britain for over 25 years was opened in Norton Street, Liverpool. This new facility, which was widely acclaimed, greatly increased the number of customers using National Express coach services from that area.

Similar increases in passenger numbers were also to be seen when even more new coach stations were opened by National Express at Dyer Street in Leeds in 1996, Harbour Parade Southampton in 1998, Manchester Central in 2002 and St James Boulevard in Newcastle-upon Tyne during Spring 2003. Discussions are also currently taking place with Birmingham City Council to replace the ageing Digbeth Coach Station.

Improvements have also been made to assist customers who want to find out about National Express services and make credit card bookings by phone and via the internet. A new Customer Contact Centre opened by the Minister of Transport John Spellar in July 2001, based in central Birmingham now offers its customers the very latest in call-centre technology. With more staff and more telephone lines than ever before, it replaces the three previous Call Centres based at Digbeth, Glasgow and Manchester. Centralising this activity on just one site offers major benefits to customers and enables it to offer a much-improved service. It will also enable it to increase the opportunities for 'remote ticketing' facilities where customers can book by phone and collect their tickets at the station prior to departure. Sixty such sites are now operational around the UK.

Dedicated airport coach services have also been identified by National Express as an important growth area. In October 1994 a newly branded service – Airlinks – specifically for the airport market, was established on the Bradford/Leeds to Heathrow/Gatwick corridor. This was followed in May 1995 with the introduction of Airlinks services on corridors between Newcastle/Nottingham to Heathrow/Gatwick, Swansea/Cardiff to Heathrow/Gatwick and Bristol to Heathrow/Gatwick. Seen in the 'Airport' version of the livery is National Express' own 310, N310VAV. *Tony Wilson*

These developments, along with the development of a computerised reservation system 'EXTRA' and an automated ticketing system 'SMART' has greatly improved the efficiency of ticketing systems for both National Express and its network of over 3,000 UK agents. Website developments have also been dramatic with both customers and ticket agents benefitting from easy access to information via the internet.

Growth

Over the decades the National Express Coach Division has continued to grow from strength to strength. Within the UK over 700 scheduled 'white coach' services now operate to around 1200 different destinations daily.

In addition National Express Shuttle services provide a low cost, high frequency shuttle service between major towns and cities. First introduced in 1994 on routes between Manchester, Liverpool and Leeds, these Shuttle services have continued to grow over the years with even more routes being introduced to/from London including those from Birmingham, Brighton, Bristol, Bournemouth, Cambridge, Southampton and Dover.

Dedicated airport coach services have also been identified by National Express as an important growth area. In October 1994 a newly branded service – Airlinks – specifically for the airport market, was established on the

Bradford/Leeds to Heathrow/Gatwick corridor. This was followed in May 1995 with the introduction of Airlinks services on corridors between Newcastle/Nottingham to Heathrow/Gatwick, Swansea/Cardiff to Heathrow/Gatwick and Bristol to Heathrow/Gatwick.

Early in 1996 the acquisition of the Flightlink brand saw the inclusion of new airport corridors from the West Midlands to Heathrow, Gatwick and Manchester airports. The re-branding of all dedicated airport corridors to Flightlink and the launch of the Flightlink network followed.

In mid-1997 Speedlink Airport Services commenced operation of Hotel Hoppa, serving all thirteen Heathrow airport hotels. This major operation, using thirty low floor buses was a major partnership between Speedlink, BAA and the Heathrow airport hoteliers, and succeeded in reducing traffic congestion in the Heathrow central area by over 30%.

Following a decision made in mid-1998 to bring together the airport operations of Speedlink Airport Services Ltd and the NEL airport services brand of Flightlink, a new company was formed on 1 January 1999 – AirLinks, The Airport Coach Company Limited which was to focus on airport-scheduled and contract bus and coach services. Operating vehicles with distinctive liveries such as Flightlink, Speedlink, Airbus and Jetlink, the airport coach service network continued to grow apace. AirLinks acquired all third party interests in the Jetlink brand, including Silverwing Transport Services, Cambridge Coach Services Ltd, Airbus and Capital Logistics, all of which provided similar coach and bus operations within the Stansted, Luton, Heathrow and Gatwick airports. AirLinks soon became the largest operator of both scheduled and contract services to BAA and the airline operators.

During this same period the Eurolines coach services into Europe also progressed well. The Eurolines network of coaches, which forms part of a much larger European coach partnership, has gradually expanded to cover over 550 different destinations. The network includes popular 'shortbreak' destinations such as Paris, Amsterdam and Brussels but also includes much longer routes to destinations as far away as Russia, Morocco and Romania.

www.nationalexpress.com

National Express was one of the first UK transport companies to recognise the importance of the internet for customers wishing to obtain travel information and to book tickets. The internet provides an easy reference point for our customers, meaning they can now get access to information and buy tickets at any time of the day, and from anywhere in the world.

And it is clearly a success with over six million people visiting the National Express website during 2002. The website address is prominently featured on all the company's literature and since 2000 the website address has also been included as part of the National Express coach livery. This all helps to ensure that even more customers know where to 'click-on'.

The company has also been successful in converting a high proportion of internet customers from 'looking to booking' with a site conversion eight times

Double-deck coaches are provided by Trathens who operate twelve Neoplan Skyliners. Pictured at Calcot interchange and showing the application of the new National Express styling is YN51XML. *Dave Heath*

higher than the industry standard. The recent roll-out of 'e-tickets', enabling customers to print tickets from their own pc printer, has meant that almost one in three customers now choose this method of purchase and has increased internet sales to well over £1m a month.

03/03/03

Perhaps the biggest change to take place within National Express in recent times occurred on 3 March 2003. It was on 03/03/03 that National Express revealed a brand new corporate identity for its business to an invited audience at the Alexandra Palace in London.

A new 'one company' logo was designed to bring together all the differing coach brands acquired by National Express over the recent years. Brands such as Flightlink, Jetlink, Speedlink, Express Shuttle and GoByCoach were now all to be amalgamated under just one name - National Express. The new logo, which retains the red, white and blue colours, has been warmly welcomed as dynamic and progressive without losing the trust and familiarity that so many passengers value.

Airlinks, which operates from three locations near London Heathrow, provides the vehicles that connect the airport with central London. The principal service is provided by Alexander-bodied Olympians, although 91, R91GTW, seen at Marble Arch is one of a pair with Northern Counties bodywork. *Mark Lyons*

The logo has now been rolled out across the National Express business and uses descriptors to differentiate specific services such as 'Shuttle', 'Airport' and 'Europe'. Another important part of the new identity is 'The Smile' factor created by the arrow linking our new red and blue circles.

Our new 'outside look' is also being supported with a new 'inside feel' to the business. The 'NX' factor as it has become known, offers seven core values that everyone in the business can follow.

"The changes made by National Express are positive and will be seen as such by the travelling public," said Rob Orchard of Coach & Bus Buyer. "It isn't until you see the new logo and livery that it occurs to you that the old familiar one had become rather stale", said Mike Ball MD of Volvo Bus. These were just two of the very favourable comments offered after the launch.

This is clearly an exciting time for National Express. With a new look, 'value for money' fares, new coach stations and helpful and professional staff – surely there's only one way to travel around Britain, to airports, and throughout Europe and that's to go by National Express.

NATIONAL EXPRESS

National Express Operations Ltd, Sipson Road, West Drayton, UB7 0HN
National Express Operations (Stansted) Ltd, Roberts House, Kilmaine Close, Cambridge, CB4 2PH

010	London - Cambridge
025	London - Gatwick - Brighton
027	London - Chichester
205	Gatwick - Poole
304	Liverpool - Weymouth
314	Cambridge - Weymouth
325	Birmingham - Manchester
420	London - Birmingham
700	Heathrow - Gatwick South
707	Northampton - Gatwick South
717	Brighton - Cambridge
727	Norwich - Gatwick
757	Oxford - Stansted
787	Cambridge - Heathrow
797	Brighton - Cambridge

A91	SH	R91GTM	Volvo Olympian		Northern Counties Palatine	BC29/9F	1998	Cambridge Coach Serv, '00
A92	SH	R92GTM	Volvo Olympian		Northern Counties Palatine	BC29/9F	1998	Cambridge Coach Serv, '00

A112-123   Volvo Olympian YN2RV18Z4   Alexander Royale   BC43/9FL   1995   London United, 2000

A112	WR	N112UHP	A115	WR	N115UHP	A118	WR	N118UHP	A121	WR	N121UHP
A113	WR	N113UHP	A116	WR	N116UHP	A119	WR	N119UHP	A122	WR	N122UHP
A114	WR	N114UHP	A117	WR	N117UHP	A120	WR	N120UHP	A123	WR	N123UHP

D1	FM	P111SAS	DAF DE33WSSB3000	Alizèe Alizèe HE	C46FT	1997
D2	FM	P222SAS	DAF DE33WSSB3000	Van Hool Alizèe HE	C46FT	1997
D3	FM	P333SAS	DAF DE33WSSB3000	Van Hool Alizèe HE	C46FT	1997
D4	FM	P444SAS	DAF DE33WSSB3000	Van Hool Alizèe HE	C46FT	1997

Northampton is the northern point of route 707, with Gatwick Airport as its southern terminus. D18, P90SAS, illustrates the Plaxton Première body, which was also adapted for National Express services as the Expressliner 2.
Dave Heath

Several of the Van Hool T9 Alizèe-bodied DAFs carry the livery of Virgin Atlantic. Seen in the scheme is D322, Y322HUA, on a Heathrow to Gatwick link. *Dave Heath*

D5-11

DAF DE33WSSB3000   Van Hool T9 Alizèe   C46FT   1999

D5	FM	T205AUA	D7	FM	T207AUA	D9	CY	T209AUA	D11	CY	T211AUA
D6	FM	T206AUA	D8	CY	T208AUA	D10	CY	T210AUA			

D12	CY	N21ARC	DAF DE33WSSB3000	Plaxton Première 350	C49FT	1996	Skill's, Nottingham, 2000
D15	CY	P50SAS	DAF DE33WSSB3000	Plaxton Première 350	C51FT	1997	
D17	CY	P70SAS	DAF DE33WSSB3000	Plaxton Première 350	C51FT	1997	
D18	CY	P80SAS	DAF DE33WSSB3000	Plaxton Première 350	C51FT	1997	
D19	CY	P90SAS	DAF DE33WSSB3000	Plaxton Première 350	C51FT	1997	

D21-25

DAF DE33WSSB3000   Plaxton Première 350   C51FT   1998

D21	FM	R100SPK	D23	FM	R300SPK	D24	FM	R400SPK	D25	FM	R500SPK
D22	FM	R200SPK									

D26	FM	W336CDN	DAF DE33WSSB3000	Plaxton Première 350	C51FT	2000
D27	FM	W337CDN	DAF DE33WSSB3000	Plaxton Première 350	C51FT	2000
D28	FM	W338CDN	DAF DE33WSSB3000	Plaxton Première 350	C51FT	2000
D29	FM	W339CDN	DAF DE33WSSB3000	Plaxton Première 350	C51FT	2000
D30	CY	P30SAS	DAF DE33WSSB3000	Plaxton Première 350	C51FT	1997

D301-331

DAF DE33WSSB3000   Van Hool T9 Alizèe   C49FT   2001   D322-31 are C35FT

D301	CY	Y301HUA	D308	FM	Y308HUA	D314	CY	Y314HUA	D324	CY	Y324HUA
D302	CY	Y302HUA	D309	FM	Y309HUA	D315	CB	Y315HUA	D326	CY	Y326HUA
D303	CY	Y303HUA	D311	CY	Y311HUA	D317	CB	Y317HUA	D327	CY	Y327HUA
D304	CY	Y304HUA	D312	CY	Y312HUA	D319	CB	Y319HUA	D329	CY	Y329HUA
D307	CY	Y307HUA	D313	CY	Y313HUA	D322	CY	Y322HUA	D331	CY	Y331HUA

S6-14

Scania K113CRB   Van Hool Alizèe SH   C45FT*   1993   *S11-15 are C35FT

S6	SN	K66SAS	S9	SN	K99SAS	S12	FM	L2SAS	S14	FM	L4SAS
S7	SN	K77SAS	S10	SN	K100SAS	S13	FM	L3SAS	S15	FM	L5SAS
S8	SN	K88SAS	S11	FM	L10SAS						

As we go to press, the first few of the Irizar Century PBs are entering service on the Birmingham to London service. The batch of fourteen, which has leather seating amongst many features, is represented by NXL4, YN04GKV, seen here near the Feltham depot. *Bill Potter*

S16-29

		Scania K113CRB			Van Hool Alizèe SH			C35FT	1996	·
S16	FM	M716KPD	S26	FM	N826DKU	S28	CB	N828DKU	S29	CB	N829DKU
S25	FM	N825DKU	S27	FM	N827DKU					

S327-898

		Scania K			Irizar Century			C49FT	2004	Bus Eireann, 2004
327	FM	W327MKY	894	FM	W894MKY	895	FM	W895MKY	898	FM	W898MKY
328	FM	W328MKY								

NXL1-14

		Scania K114EB4			Irizar Century PB			C49FT	2004	
1	FM	YN04GKL	5	FM	YN04GKY	9	FM	YN04GPF	12	FM	YN04GPU
2	FM	YN04GKP	6	FM	YN04GKX	10	FM	YN04GPJ	13	FM	YN04GPV
3	FM	YN04GKU	7	FM	YN04GLF	11	FM	YN04GPK	14	FM	YN04GPX
4	FM	YN04GKV	8	FM	YN04GLJ					

V21-25

		Volvo B10M-62			Plaxton Première 350			C51FT	1995	
V21	CB	M721KPD	V23	CB	M723KPD	V24	CB	M724KPD	V25	CB	M725KPD
V22	CB	M722KPD								

V26-43

		Volvo B12B			Plaxton Panther			C49FT	2003	
V26	FM	LK53KVO	V31	FM	LK53KWD	V35	FM	LK53KVY	V39	FM	LK53KVU
V27	FM	LK53KXB	V32	FM	LK53KWB	V36	FM	LK53KVX	V41	FM	LK53KVT
V28	FM	LK53KXA	V33	FM	LK53KWA	V37	FM	LK53KVW	V42	FM	LK53KVR
V29	FM	LK53KWF	V34	FM	LK53KVZ	V38	FM	LK53KVV	V43	FM	LK53KVP
V30	FM	LK53KWE								

V40-90

		Volvo B10M-62			Plaxton Première 350			C51FT	2000	Skill's, Nottingham, 2000
V40	CY	N40SLK	V60	CY	N60SLK	V80	CY	N80SLK	V90	CY	N90SLK
V50	CY	N50SLK	V70	CY	N70SLK					

V823	CB	Y823HHE	Volvo B10M-62			Plaxton Paragon		C49FT	2001	Memories for Tomorrow, '02
V824	CB	Y824HHE	Volvo B10M-62			Plaxton Paragon		C49FT	2001	Memories for Tomorrow, '02
V825	CB	Y825HHE	Volvo B10M-62			Plaxton Paragon		C49FT	2001	Memories for Tomorrow, '02

71-76

Dennis Dart SLF   Plaxton Pointer 2   N33D   1999

71	WR	T71WWV	**73**	WR	T73WWV	**75**	WR	T75WWV	**76**	WR	T76WWV
72	WR	T72WWV	**74**	WR	T74WWV						

226-251

Volvo B6LE   Wright Crusader   NC28F   1997

226	WR	P226AAP	**233**	WR	P233AAP	**240**	WR	P240AAP	**246**	WR	P246AAP
227	WR	P227AAP	**234**	WR	P234AAP	**241**	WR	P241AAP	**247**	WR	P247AAP
228	WR	P228AAP	**235**	WR	P235AAP	**242**	WR	P242AAP	**248**	WR	P248AAP
229	WR	P229AAP	**236**	WR	P236AAP	**243**	WR	P243AAP	**249**	WR	P249AAP
230	WR	P230AAP	**237**	WR	P237AAP	**244**	WR	P244AAP	**250**	WR	P250AAP
231	WR	P231AAP	**238**	WR	P238AAP	**245**	WR	P245AAP	**251**	WR	P251AAP
232	WR	P232AAP	**239**	WR	P239AAP						

301-315

Volvo B10M-62   Plaxton Première 350   C52F   1994-97

301	CB	M301BAV	**305**	CB	M305BAV	**309**	SH	N309VAV	**313**	SH	P313CVE
302	CB	M302BAV	**306**	CB	M306BAV	**310**	SH	N310VAV	**314**	SH	P314CVE
303	CB	M303BAV	**307**	SH	M307BAV	**311**	SH	N311VAV	**315**	SH	P315DVE
304	CB	M304BAV	**308**	SH	M308BAV	**312**	SH	N312VAV			

320	CB	S320VNM	Volvo B10M-66 SE	Plaxton Première 350	C48FT	1999	
322	CB	S322VNM	Volvo B10M-66 SE	Plaxton Première 350	C48FT	1999	
323	CB	S323VNM	Volvo B10M-66 SE	Plaxton Première 350	C48FT	1999	
324	CB	S324VNM	Volvo B10M-66 SE	Plaxton Première 350	C48FT	1999	
325	CB	T325APP	Volvo B10M-62	Plaxton Première 350	C52FL	1999	

1110	SH	M563XFY	Mercedes-Benz 208D	Concept	M8	1995	Capital, West Drayton, 2000
1129	SH	M537XFY	Mercedes-Benz 208D	Concept	M8	1995	Capital, West Drayton, 2000
1131	SH	N648DFY	Mercedes-Benz 208D	Concept	M8	1996	Capital, West Drayton, 2000
1165	SH	W922PCD	Volvo B7R	Plaxton Prima	C53F	2000	
1166	CY	W923PCD	Volvo B7R	Plaxton Prima	C53F	2000	
1167	CY	W924PCD	Volvo B7R	Plaxton Prima	C53F	2000	
1168	CY	W926PCD	Volvo B7R	Plaxton Prima	C53F	2000	

Ancillary vehicles

1091	FM	H395SYG	DAF SB220LC550	Optare Delta	TV	1990	Capital, West Drayton, 2000
1092	FM	H396SYG	DAF SB220LC550	Optare Delta	TV	1990	Capital, West Drayton, 2000
1093	FM	H843UUA	DAF SB220LC550	Optare Delta	TV	1990	Capital, West Drayton, 2000

Details of the other coaches and Airlinks buses in this fleet may be found in The South East Bus Handbook.

The 2003 intake of coaches for the Airlinks service comprised Volvo B12Bs with Plaxton Paragon bodywork. The B12B is Volvo's rear-engined model with the B12M having a centrally mounted underfloor engine. LK53KVR is shown in Golders Green. *Mark Lyons*

AMBASSADOR TRAVEL

Ambassador Travel Ltd, James Watt Close, Gapton Hall, Great Yarmouth, NR31 0NX

308	Great Yarmouth - Birmingham
420	London - Birmingham
495	London - Cromer
496	London - Cromer
497	London - Great Yarmouth

141	M743KJU	Volvo B10M-62	Plaxton Premiére 350	C51F	1995	
148	P411MDT	Volvo B10M-62	Plaxton Premiére 350	C48FT	1997	
149	P412MDT	Volvo B10M-62	Plaxton Premiére 350	C46FT	1997	
151	R85DVF	Volvo B10M-62	Plaxton Premiére 350	C51F	1998	
195	P803BLJ	Volvo B10M-62	Plaxton Premiére 350	C49FT	1997	Excelsior, Bournemouth, '01
196	FN52HRG	Volvo B10M-62	Plaxton Paragon	C49FT	2002	
197	FN52HRM	Volvo B10M-62	Plaxton Paragon	C49FT	2002	

Details of the coaches in this fleet may be found in The Eastern Bus Handbook

ANDERSONS

E M & P Anderson, Hunslet Business Park, 76 Goodwin Street, Leeds, LS10 1NY

320	Bradford - Birmingham
660	Bradford - Skegness

No vehicles are contracted in National Express colours. The vehicles used on the services are selected from the main fleet.

APPLEGATES

F Applegate, Heathfield Garage, Newport, Berkeley, Gloucester, GL13 9LP

040	Bristol - London
318	Bristol - Birmingham

No vehicles are contracted to operate in National Express colours. The vehicles used on the services are selected from the main fleet. Details of the vehicles in this fleet may be found in The South West Bus Handbook

ARRIVA MIDLANDS

Arriva Fox County Ltd, PO Box 613, Melton Road, Thurmaston, Leicester, LE4 8ZN

302	Swansea - Bristol					
348	Leicester - Bristol					
440	London - Buxton - Leicester					
440	London - Burton-on-Trent					
440	London - Derby					

3201	P201RWR	DAF DE33WSSB3000	Van Hool Alizèe	C49FT	1997	First Edinburgh, 2001
3202	YJ04BKF	VDL Bus SB4000	Van Hool T9 Alizèe	C49FT	2003	
3203	YJ53VFY	DAF DE40XSSB4000	Van Hool T9 Alizèe	C49FT	2003	
3204	YJ03PFX	DAF DE40XSSB4000	Van Hool T9 Alizèe	C49FT	2003	
3205	P205RWR	DAF DE33WSSB3000	Van Hool Alizèe	C49FT	1997	Arriva Yorkshire, 2000
3209	T209XVO	DAF DE33WSSB3000	Van Hool T9 Alizèe	C51FT	1999	
3210	T119AUA	DAF DE33WSSB3000	Van Hool T9 Alizèe	C51FT	1999	
3211	662NKR	Volvo B10M-62	Plaxton Expressliner 2	C49FT	1996	

Previous Registration
662NKR   N211TBC

Details of the other vehicles in this fleet may be found in the annual Arriva Bus Handbook

As well as one of the major European bus operators, Arriva is the importer of VDL Bus chassis into Britain. VDL is the new name for DAF Bus, and the coachworks in the Group include VDL Jonckheere and VDL Berkhof. For National Express duties, Arriva has selected the Van Hool T9 Alizèe bodywork for its own coaches. Arriva Midlands' main route is that connecting the capital with Leicester, and 3209, T209XVO, is seen on that service. *Dave Heath*

ARRIVA NORTH EAST

Arriva North East Ltd, Arriva House, Admiral Way, Sunderland, SR3 3XP

032		Southampton - London			
326		Manchester Airport - Newcastle			
425		Ashington - Newcastle - London			

141	V141EJR	DAF DE33WSSB3000	Van Hool T9 Alizèe	C44FT	1999
142	V142EJR	DAF DE33WSSB3000	Van Hool T9 Alizèe	C44FT	1999
143	X143WNL	DAF DE33WSSB3000	Van Hool T9 Alizèe	C49FT	2000
144	X144WNL	DAF DE33WSSB3000	Van Hool T9 Alizèe	C49FT	2000
145	NL52XZV	DAF DE40XSSB4000	Van Hool T9 Alizèe	C49FT	2002
146	NL52XZW	DAF DE40XSSB4000	Van Hool T9 Alizèe	C49FT	2002
147	NL52XZX	DAF DE40XSSB4000	Van Hool T9 Alizèe	C49FT	2002
148	NL52XZY	DAF DE40XSSB4000	Van Hool T9 Alizèe	C49FT	2002

Details of the other vehicles in this fleet may be found in the annual Arriva Bus Handbook

Arriva North East's principal service connects the Newcastle area to London with four daily departures each way. Seen in London at the start of a return leg to Ashington is 147, NL52XZX. *Dave Heath*

BEBB

Bebb Travel plc, The Coach Station, Llantwit Fardre, Rhondda Cynon Taf, CF38 2HB

320	Cardiff - Bradford
321	Aberdare - Bradford
502	London - Ilfracombe
509	London - Aberdare
509	London - Cardiff
536	Edinburgh - Cardiff

Y93HTX	Volvo B10M-62	Plaxton Paragon	C49FT	2001
Y94HTX	Volvo B10M-62	Plaxton Paragon	C49FT	2001
Y96HTX	Volvo B10M-62	Plaxton Paragon	C49FT	2001
Y97HTX	Volvo B10M-62	Plaxton Paragon	C49FT	2001
CN51XNU	Volvo B12M	Plaxton Paragon	C49FT	2002
CN51XNV	Volvo B12M	Plaxton Paragon	C49FT	2002
CN51XNW	Volvo B12M	Plaxton Paragon	C49FT	2002
CN51XNX	Volvo B12M	Plaxton Paragon	C49FT	2002
CN51XNY	Volvo B12M	Plaxton Paragon	C49FT	2002
CN51XNZ	Volvo B12M	Plaxton Paragon	C49FT	2002
CN53NWB	Volvo B12M	Plaxton Paragon	C49FT	2004
CN53NWC	Volvo B12M	Plaxton Paragon	C49FT	2004
CN04NFD	Volvo B12M	Plaxton Paragon	C49FT	2004
CN04NFE	Volvo B12M	Plaxton Paragon	C49FT	2004
CN04NFF	Volvo B12M	Plaxton Paragon	C49FT	2004
CN04NFG	Volvo B12M	Plaxton Paragon	C49FT	2004

Details of the other vehicles in this fleet may be found in The Welsh Bus Handbook.

New arrivals with Bebbs for National Express work are further Plaxton Paragon-bodied Volvo B12Ms. Seen in Cardiff, CN04NFG was preparing to head for London. *Dave Heath*

BENNETT'S

B A & D B Bennett, The Garage, Athlone Road, Warrington, WA2 8JJ

540	Manchester - London
664	Preston - Skegness

No vehicles are contracted to operate in National Express colours. The vehicles used on the service are selected from the main fleet. Details of the vehicles in this fleet may be found in The North West Bus Handbook

BIRMINGHAM COACH COMPANY

Birmingham Coach Co Ltd, Cross Quays Business Park, Hallbridge Way, Tividale, B69 3HY

240	Bradford - Gatwick
310	Birmingham - Bradford
325	Birmingham - Manchester
341	Birmingham - Burnham
387	Blackpool - Coventry
412	Great Malvern - London
420	London - Wolverhampton
420	London - Aberystwyth
420	London - Birmingham
545	London - Pwllheli
777	Birmingham - Stansted

One of the long-established contractors for National Express is the Birmingham Coach Company. During 2003, six further DAF coaches with the latest Van Hool Alizée bodywork entered the fleet. The Alizée is now mostly produced for the right-hand drive British and Irish markets, with most left-hand drive sales comprising the integral coaches. YJ03PNN is seen on route 240 that connects Bradford with Gatwick.
Dave Heath

30	W30DTS	Scania K124IB4	Van Hool Alizée	C44FT	2000	Durham Travel, 2003
31	W431RBB	Scania K124IB4	Van Hool Alizée	C44FT	2000	Durham Travel, 2003
32	W432RBB	Scania K124IB4	Van Hool Alizée	C44FT	2000	Durham Travel, 2003
33	T949JUG	DAF DE33WSSB3000	Van Hool T9 Alizée	C44FT	1999	Arriva Yorkshire, 2003
34	T178FUM	DAF DE33WSSB3000	Van Hool T9 Alizée	C44FT	1999	Arriva Yorkshire, 2003
35	T174FUM	DAF DE33WSSB3000	Van Hool T9 Alizée	C44FT	1999	Arriva Yorkshire, 2003
36	T36EUA	DAF DE33WSSB3000	Van Hool T9 Alizée	C44FT	1999	Arriva Yorkshire, 2003
37	T37EUA	DAF DE33WSSB3000	Van Hool T9 Alizée	C44FT	1999	Arriva Yorkshire, 2003
38	T38EUA	DAF DE33WSSB3000	Van Hool T9 Alizée	C44FT	1999	Arriva Yorkshire, 2003
	X421WVO	Scania K124IB4	Van Hool T9 Alizée	C49FT	2001	
	X422WVO	Scania K124IB4	Van Hool T9 Alizée	C49FT	2001	
	X423WVO	Scania K124IB4	Van Hool T9 Alizée	C49FT	2001	
	YP02AAV	Scania K114IB4	Van Hool T9 Alizée	C49FT	2002	
	YP02AAX	Scania K114IB4	Van Hool T9 Alizée	C49FT	2002	
	YP52KRZ	Volvo B12B	Plaxton Paragon	C49FT	2003	
	YJ03PGX	DAF DE40XSSB4000	Van Hool T9 Alizée	C49FT	2003	
	YJ03PGY	DAF DE40XSSB4000	Van Hool T9 Alizée	C49FT	2003	
	YJ03PGZ	DAF DE40XSSB4000	Van Hool T9 Alizée	C49FT	2003	
	YJ03PKK	DAF DE40XSSB4000	Van Hool T9 Alizée	C49FT	2003	
	YJ03PNN	DAF DE40XSSB4000	Van Hool T9 Alizée	C49FT	2003	
	YJ53VHF	DAF DE40XSSB4000	Van Hool T9 Alizée	C49FT	2003	

Previous registrations:

T174FUM	A4YBG		T949JUG	A1YBG
T178FUM	A2YBG			

Details of the other vehicles in this fleet may be found in the West Midlands Bus Handbook.

BIRMINGHAM INTERNATIONAL

Claribel Coaches Ltd, 10 Fortnum Close, Tile Cross, Birmingham, B33 0JT

342	Birmingham - Newquay
397	Blackpool - Leicester

No vehicles are contracted to operate in National Express colours. The vehicles used on the service are selected from the main fleet. Details of the vehicles in this fleet may be found in the West Midlands Bus Handbook.

Birmingham Coach Company operate X422WVO, a Scania K124 with Van Hool T9 Alizée bodywork. It is seen in Park Lane, London, while operating a journey on the 420 service.
Tony Wilson

BOURNEMOUTH TRANSPORT

Bournemouth Transport Ltd, Transport Depot, Mallard Road, Bournemouth, BH8 9PN

032	Bournemouth - London	
032	Southampton - London	
035	London - Poole - Weymouth	
035	Swanage - London	
652	Southampton - London	

310	HF53OBG	Volvo B12B	TransBus Paragon	C49FT	2003	
311	HF53OBH	Volvo B12B	TransBus Paragon	C49FT	2003	
312		Volvo B12B	Caetano Enigma	C49FT	On Order	
313		Volvo B12B	Caetano Enigma	C49FT	On Order	
314		Volvo B12B	Caetano Enigma	C49FT	On Order	
326	R326NRU	Volvo B10M-62	Van Hool T9 Alizée	C49FT	1998	
327	R327NRU	Volvo B10M-62	Van Hool T9 Alizée	C49FT	1998	
329	R329NRU	Volvo B10M-62	Van Hool T9 Alizée	C49FT	1998	
330	T330AFX	Volvo B10M-62	Van Hool T9 Alizée	C49FT	1999	
331	T331AFX	Volvo B10M-62	Van Hool T9 Alizée	C49FT	1999	
338	R338NEV	Volvo B10M-62	Berkhof Axial 50	C49FT	1998	?
354	R354NRU	Volvo B10M-62	Van Hool T9 Alizée	C48FT	1998	
355	R355NRU	Volvo B10M-62	Van Hool T9 Alizée	C48FT	1998	
381	W381UEL	Scania L94IB	Van Hool T9 Alizée	C49FT	2000	
382	W382UEL	Scania L94IB	Van Hool T9 Alizée	C49FT	2000	
383	W383UEL	Scania L94IB	Van Hool T9 Alizée	C49FT	2000	
384	W384UEL	Scania L94IB	Van Hool T9 Alizée	C49FT	2000	

Details of the other vehicles in this fleet may be found in the South West Bus Handbook.

National Express Shuttle provides a low cost, high frequency service between major towns and cities. Introduced in 1994 on routes between Manchester, Liverpool and Leeds these Shuttle services have continued to grow over the years with even more routes being introduced to/from London including those from Birmingham, Brighton, Bristol, Bournemouth, Cambridge, Southampton and Dover. Seen with Shuttle lettering is Bournemouth's 384, W384UEL, a Scania L94. *Dave Heath*

BRUCE'S

J Bruce, 40 Main Street, Salsburgh, ML7 4LA

538	Glasgow - Manchester Airport
539	Edinburgh - Bournemouth
591	Edinburgh - London

V10NAT	Bova FHD12.340	Bova Futura	C46FT	2000
X20NAT	Bova FHD12.340	Bova Futura	C46FT	2001
BC51NAT	Bova FHD12.340	Bova Futura	C48FT	2002
BC54NAT	Bova FHD12.340	Bova Futura	C48FT	On order

Details of the other vehicles in this fleet may be found in the Scottish Bus Handbook.

BURTON'S

Burton's Coaches Ltd, Duddery Hill, Haverhill, Suffolk, CB9 8DR

| 010 | London - Cambridge | 027 | London - Chichester |
| 010 | London - Kings Lynn | 314 | Cambridge - Birmingham |

YU04XFB	Volvo B12B	TransBus Panther	C49FT	2004
YU04XFC	Volvo B12B	TransBus Panther	C49FT	2004
YU04XFD	Volvo B12B	TransBus Panther	C49FT	2004
RK04BWU	Volvo B12B	TransBus Panther	C49FT	2004
	Volvo B12B	TransBus Panther	C49FT	2004
	Volvo B12B	TransBus Panther	C49FT	2004
	Volvo B12B	TransBus Panther	C49FT	2004
	Volvo B12B	TransBus Panther	C49FT	2004

Details of the other vehicles in this fleet may be found in The Eastern Bus Handbook

BUZZLINES

Buzzlines Ltd, G1 Lympne Industrial Park, Lympne, Hythe, CT21 4LR

| 650 | Dover - London |

No vehicles are contracted to operate in National Express colours. The vehicles used on the service are selected from the main fleet. Details of the vehicles in this fleet may be found in The South East Bus Handbook

CASTLE COACHES

Castle Coaches Ltd, 5 Queens Crescent, Waterlooville, PO8 9NB

| 668 | London - Bognor Regis |

No vehicles are contracted to operate in National Express colours. The vehicles used on the service are selected from the main fleet.

CHALFONT

Chalfont Coaches of Harrow Ltd, 200 Featherstone Road, Southall, UB2 5AQ

010	London - Cambridge	420	London - Birmingham
025	London - Brighton	440	London - Leicester
035	London - Bournemouth	460	London - Coventry
040	London - Bristol	509	London - Cardiff
412	London - Gloucester	560	London - Sheffield

No vehicles are contracted to operate in National Express colours. The vehicles used on the service are selected from the main fleet. Details of the vehicles in this fleet may be found in The London Bus Handbook.

R W CHENERY

PG Garnham, The Garage, Dickleburgh, Diss, Norfolk, IP21 4NJ

490	London - Great Yarmouth		490	London - Norwich		
K127OCT	Setra S215 HD	Setra Tornado	C44FT	1994	
R303EEX	Setra S250	Setra Special	C44FT	1998	
R304EEX	Setra S250	Setra Special	C44FT	1998	
R39AWO	Setra S250	Setra Special	C44FT	1998	Bebb, Llantwit Fardre, 2000

Previous registration
K127OCT   RYG684

Details of the other vehicles in this fleet may be found in The Eastern Bus Handbook.

CLYNNOG & TREFOR

Clynnog & Trefor Motor Co. Ltd, The Garage, Trefor, Gwynedd, LL54 5HP.

380	Llandudno - Manchester
544	Llandudno - Birmingham
662	Liverpool - Skegness

No vehicles are contracted to operate in National Express colours. The vehicles used on the service are selected from the main fleet. Details of the vehicles in this fleet may be found in The Welsh Bus Handbook.

COUNTRY TRAVEL

M Patrick, Church Street, Saxmundham, IP17 1EP

497	London – Great Yarmouth

No vehicles are contracted to operate in National Express colours. The vehicles used on the service are selected from the main fleet.

DUNN-LINE

Dunn-Line Holdings Ltd, The Coach Station, Park Lane, Basford, Nottingham, NG6 0DW

024	Eastbourne - London
210	Wolverhampton - Gatwick
210	Birmingham - Gatwick
230	Mansfield - Gatwick
330	Nottingham - Birmingham
342	Nottingham - St Ives
380	Newcastle - Leeds
426	South Shields - London
450	Nottingham - London
460	Lichfield - London
481	Felixstowe - London
538	Birmingham - Edinburgh
561	Bradford - London
561	Knaresborough - London
561	York - London
563	Whitby - London
675	Stoke - Minehead
591	Edinburgh - London

Chenery's contributions to National Express are four Setra coaches. Pictured in Norwich, on route 490 is R304EEX, an S250 Special and a model produced specifically for the British market.
Mark Doggett

26	S26DTS	Scania K124IB4	Van Hool T9 Alizée	C44FT	1999	Durham Travel, 2002
27	S27DTS	Scania K124IB4	Van Hool T9 Alizée	C44FT	1999	Durham Travel, 2002
28	YR52VFA	Scania K124IB4	Van Hool T9 Alizée	C49FT	2003	
29	YR52VFB	Scania K124IB4	Van Hool T9 Alizée	C49FT	2003	
30	YR52VFC	Scania K124IB4	Irizar Century 12.35	C49FT	2003	
31	YN03DGE	Scania K124IB4	Irizar Century 12.35	C49FT	2003	
32	YN03DFZ	Scania K124IB4	Irizar Century 12.35	C49FT	2003	
33	NK51ORJ	Scania K124IB4	Van Hool T9 Alizée	C49FT	2001	Durham Travel, 2002
34	NK51ORL	Scania K124IB4	Van Hool T9 Alizée	C49FT	2001	Durham Travel, 2002
35	NK51ORN	Scania K124IB4	Van Hool T9 Alizée	C49FT	2001	Durham Travel, 2002
36	NK51ORO	Scania K124IB4	Van Hool T9 Alizée	C49FT	2001	Durham Travel, 2002
38	ECZ9138	Volvo B10M-62	Plaxton Excalibur	C49FT	1999	
39	ECZ9139	Volvo B10M-62	Plaxton Excalibur	C49FT	1999	
40	T39CNN	Volvo B10M-62	Plaxton Excalibur	C49FT	1999	
81	W381PRC	Volvo B10M-62	Plaxton Excalibur	C49FT	2000	
82	W382PRC	Volvo B10M-62	Plaxton Excalibur	C49FT	2000	
83	W383PRC	Volvo B10M-62	Plaxton Excalibur	C49FT	2000	
84	W384PRC	Volvo B10M-62	Plaxton Excalibur	C49FT	2000	
85	W385PRC	Volvo B10M-62	Plaxton Excalibur	C49FT	2000	
86	W386PRC	Volvo B10M-62	Plaxton Excalibur	C49FT	2000	
87	W387PRC	Volvo B10M-62	Plaxton Excalibur	C49FT	2000	
88	W388PRC	Volvo B10M-62	Plaxton Excalibur	C49FT	2000	
89	W389PRC	Volvo B10M-62	Plaxton Excalibur	C49FT	2000	
	S295WOA	Volvo B10M-66SE	Plaxton Expressliner 2	C44FT	1999	Flights, Birmingham, 2002
	S296WOA	Volvo B10M-66SE	Plaxton Expressliner 2	C44FT	1999	Flights, Birmingham, 2002
	S297WOA	Volvo B10M-66SE	Plaxton Expressliner 2	C44FT	1998	Flights, Birmingham, 2002
	S298WOA	Volvo B10M-66SE	Plaxton Expressliner 2	C44FT	1998	Flights, Birmingham, 2002
	S364OOB	Volvo B10M-66SE	Plaxton Expressliner 2	C44FT	1998	Flights, Birmingham, 2002
	S365OOB	Volvo B10M-66SE	Plaxton Expressliner 2	C44FT	1998	Flights, Birmingham, 2002
	V447EAL	Volvo B10M-62	Plaxton Expressliner 2	C44FT	1999	Flights, Birmingham, 2002
	V448EAL	Volvo B10M-62	Plaxton Expressliner 2	C44FT	1999	Flights, Birmingham, 2002
	V449EAL	Volvo B10M-62	Plaxton Expressliner 2	C44FT	1999	Flights, Birmingham, 2002
	A8FTG	Volvo B10M-66SE	Plaxton Excalibur	C44FT	2000	Flight's, Birmingham, 2002
0401	FA04LJK	Volvo B12B	Plaxton Panther	C49FT	2004	
0402		Volvo B12B	Plaxton Panther	C49FT	2004	
0403		Volvo B12B	Plaxton Panther	C49FT	2004	
0404		Volvo B12B	Plaxton Panther	C49FT	2004	
0405		Volvo B12B	Plaxton Panther	C49FT	2004	
0406		Volvo B12B	Plaxton Panther	C49FT	2004	
0407		Volvo B12B	Plaxton Panther	C49FT	2004	
0408		Volvo B12B	Plaxton Panther	C49FT	2004	
0409		Volvo B12B	Plaxton Panther	C49FT	2004	
0410		Volvo B12B	Plaxton Panther	C49FT	2004	
0411		Volvo B12B	Plaxton Panther	C49FT	2004	
0412		Volvo B12B	Plaxton Panther	C49FT	2004	
0413		Volvo B12B	Plaxton Panther	C49FT	2004	
0414		Volvo B12B	Plaxton Panther	C49FT	2004	
0415		Volvo B12B	Plaxton Panther	C49FT	2004	
0416		Volvo B12B	Plaxton Panther	C49FT	2004	
0417		Volvo B12B	Plaxton Panther	C49FT	2004	
0418		Volvo B12B	Plaxton Panther	C49FT	2004	
0419		Volvo B12B	Plaxton Panther	C49FT	2004	

Previous registrations

ECZ9138	T37CNN	ECZ9139	T38CNN

Details of the other vehicles in this fleet may be found in The East Midlands Bus Handbook

EAST YORKSHIRE

East Yorkshire Motor Services Ltd, 252 Anlaby Road, Hull, HU3 2RS

040	Bristol - London	
322	Hull - Swansea	
322	Brecon - Scarborough	
390	Manchester - Hull	
562	London - Hull	
562	London - Beverley	

38	3277KH	Volvo B10M-60	Plaxton Expressliner 2	C49FT	2000
39	V839JAT	Volvo B10M-60	Plaxton Expressliner 2	C49FT	2000
40	V840JAT	Volvo B10M-60	Plaxton Expressliner 2	C49FT	2000
41	V841JAT	Volvo B10M-60	Plaxton Expressliner 2	C49FT	2000
42	V842JAT	Volvo B10M-60	Plaxton Expressliner 2	C49FT	2000
43	V843JAT	Volvo B10M-60	Plaxton Expressliner 2	C49FT	2000
44	W844SKH	Volvo B10M-60	Plaxton Expressliner 2	C44FT	2000
45	Y445XAT	Volvo B10M	Plaxton Paragon	C49FT	2000
46	YX02JFY	Volvo B12M	Plaxton Paragon	C49FT	2002

Previous registration

3277KH	V838JAT

Details of the other vehicles in this fleet may be found in The Yorkshire Bus Handbook

The Scottish fleet of Bruce's provides three Bova Futura coaches for National Express service. One of its routes connects Edinburgh with Bournemouth. Pictured at Penrith rail station, BC51NAT is seen on a southbound journey. *Tony Wilson*

EDWARDS

L J Edwards, Bellbanks Corner, Mill Road, Hailsham, BN27 2AH

024	London - Eastbourne

No vehicles are contracted to operate in National Express colours. The vehicles used on the service are selected from the main fleet.

EXCALIBUR

Excalibur Coaches Ltd, 1A Brabourn Grove, London, SE15 2BS

540	Manchester - London	550	London - Liverpool
551	Liverpool - London		

No vehicles are contracted to operate in National Express colours. The vehicles used on the service are selected from the main fleet. Details of the vehicles in this fleet may be found in The London Bus Handbook

EXCELSIOR

Excelsior Coaches Ltd, Bournemouth Sands Hotel, West Cliff Gdns, Bournemouth, BH2 5HR

035	Bournemouth - London	205	Poole - Heathrow Airport

437	A3XCL	Volvo B10M-62	Plaxton Excalibur	C44FT	1998
805	A9XCL	Volvo B10M-62	Plaxton Paragon	C44FT	2000
905	A7XCL	Volvo B10M-62	Plaxton Paragon	C44FT	2000
906	A8XCL	Volvo B10M-62	Plaxton Paragon	C44FT	2000
907	FN03DYA	Volvo B12B	Jonckheere Mistral 50	C44FT	2003
908	FN03DYB	Volvo B12B	Jonckheere Mistral 50	C44FT	2003

Previous registrations:

A3XCL	XEL31, S809DRU	A7XCL	X852WLJ

Excelsior added two Jonckheere-bodied coaches in 2003. Seen at rest at London Heathrow is Volvo B10B FN03DYB.
Dave Heath

FIRST

First Somerset & Avon Ltd, Oldmixon, Weston-Super-Mare, BS24 9AY (SA)
First Cymru Ltd, Heol Gwyrosydd, Penlan, Swansea, SA5 7BN (C)
First Southern National Ltd, Lawrence Hill, Bristol, BS5 0AZ (SN)
First Devon & Cornwall Ltd, The Ride, Chelson Meadow, Plymouth, PL4 6ZB (DC)

040	London - Brean Sands	SN
040	London - Bristol	SN
200	Bristol - Gatwick Airport	SN
201	Gatwick - Swansea	C
302	Bristol - Swansea	C
302	Bristol - Cardiff	SN
310	Birmingham - Bradford	SN (to 9/04)
315	Heston - Eastbourne	DC
316	Pertsmouth - Perranporth	DC
318	Bristol - Liverpool	SN
325	Birmingham - Manchester	SN (to 9/04)
328	Plymouth - Rochdale	DC
330	Penzance - Nottingham	DC
336	Penzance - Edinburgh	DC
339	Grimsby - Westward Ho!	DC

Route 420 between Wolverhampton and London is to receive new Scania coaches during September 2004 and the operation will transfer to National Express themselves, with First gaining new services. The current coaches are expected to be reallocated within First. Plaxton Paragon 20535, WM03BXP, is seen in Wolverhampton with buses from National Express Group's Travel West Midlands fleet in the background.
Mark Doggett

341	Paignton - Burnley	SN					
342	Newquay - Bristol	DC					
343	Leeds - Newquay	DC					
402	London - Frome	SA					
403	London - Bath	SA					
403	London - Bath Spa	DC					
403	London - Street	SA					
404	London - Penzance	DC					
412	London - Worcester	SN (from 9/04)					
412	London - Gloucester	SN (from 9/04)					
420	London - Birmingham	SN (to 9/04)					
420	London - Wolverhampton	SN (to 9/04)					
460	London - Stratford-upon-Avon	SN					
500	London - Penzance	DC					
502	Bideford - London	DC					
504	London - Penzance	DC					
505	London - Penzance	DC					
508	London - Swansea	C					
508	London - Llanelli	C					
508	London - Haverfordwest	C					
528	Blackpool - Birmingham - Haverfordwest	C					
545	London - Pwllheli	SN					
707	Northampton - Gatwick South						

20404	BB	R304JAF	Volvo B10M-62	Plaxton Expressliner 2	C44FT	1998	
20405	BB	R305JAF	Volvo B10M-62	Plaxton Expressliner 2	C44FT	1998	
20407	DC	R307JAF	Volvo B10M-62	Plaxton Expressliner 2	C44FT	1998	
20408	DC	R308JAF	Volvo B10M-62	Plaxton Expressliner 2	C44FT	1998	
20409	DC	R309JAF	Volvo B10M-62	Plaxton Expressliner 2	C44FT	1998	
20410	DC	R310JAF	Volvo B10M-62	Plaxton Expressliner 2	C44FT	1998	
20411	DC	S311SCV	Volvo B10M-62	Plaxton Expressliner 2	C44FT	1998	
20412	DC	S312SCV	Volvo B10M-62	Plaxton Expressliner 2	C44FT	1998	
20413	DC	S313SCV	Volvo B10M-62	Plaxton Expressliner 2	C44FT	1998	
20416	DC	T316KCV	Volvo B10M-62	Plaxton Expressliner 2	C44FT	1999	
20419	C	P804BLJ	Volvo B10M-62	Plaxton Expressliner 2	C44FT	1997	Excelsior, Bournemouth, '00
20421	DC	P521PRL	Volvo B10M-62	Van Hool Alizée HE	C44FT	1996	
20424	C	T64BHY	Volvo B10M-62	Plaxton Expressliner 2	C44FT	1999	
20428	C	T948UEU	Volvo B10M-62	Plaxton Expressliner 2	C44FT	1999	
20429	C	S104JGB	Volvo B10M-62	Plaxton Expressliner 2	C49FT	1998	Trathen's, Plymouth, 2003
20430	C	S105JGB	Volvo B10M-62	Plaxton Expressliner 2	C49FT	1998	Trathen's, Plymouth, 2003
20431	C	T868RGA	Volvo B10M-62	Plaxton Expressliner 2	C49FT	1999	Trathen's, Plymouth, 2003
20432	C	T869RGA	Volvo B10M-62	Plaxton Expressliner 2	C49FT	1999	Trathen's, Plymouth, 2003
20435	DC	M765CWS	Volvo B10M-62	Plaxton Expressliner 2	C49FT	1994	
20444	DC	P234BFJ	Volvo B10M-62	Plaxton Expressliner 2	C50FT	1996	

The 2003 intake of Paragon coaches for First featured lifts to allow access for wheelchair-bound passengers. The allocation was initially split between Swansea and Bristol. Here 20539, CU03AVD, from Swansea, is seen on the Gatwick Service.
Dave Heath

Between 2003 and mid-2004 coaches built by Plaxton, Alexander and Dennis used their parent's TransBus name for products. Thus Shuttle lettering is seen here on TransBus Paragon 20541, WX53PFG, seen rounding Hyde Park Corner. *Tony Wilson*

20454	LH	P944RWS	Volvo B10M-62	Plaxton Expressliner 2	C46FT	1996
20455	LH	P945RWS	Volvo B10M-62	Plaxton Expressliner 2	C48FT	1996
20456	LH	P946RWS	Volvo B10M-62	Plaxton Expressliner 2	C49FT	1996
20457	LH	R813HWS	Volvo B10M-62	Plaxton Expressliner 2	C49FT	1997
20458	LH	R814HWS	Volvo B10M-62	Plaxton Expressliner 2	C49FT	1997
20459	LH	R943LHT	Volvo B10M-62	Plaxton Expressliner 2	C44FT	1998
20460	LH	T310AHY	Volvo B10M-62	Plaxton Expressliner 2	C44FT	1999
20461	LH	X191HFB	Volvo B10M-62	Plaxton Expressliner 2	C44FT	2000
20462	LH	X192HFB	Volvo B10M-62	Plaxton Expressliner 2	C44FT	2000
20463	LH	X193HFB	Volvo B10M-62	Plaxton Expressliner 2	C44FT	2000
20464	LH	X194HFB	Volvo B10M-62	Plaxton Expressliner 2	C44FT	2000

20510-20533

Volvo B12M · Plaxton Paragon · C44FTL · 2001-02

20510	SN	WX51AJU	20516	SA	WV02EUT	20522	SN	WV52FAO	20528	DC	WK52SVU
20511	SN	WX51AJV	20517	SA	WV02EUU	20523	SN	WX52FCX	20529	DC	WK52SVV
20512	SN	WX51AJY	20518	DC	WK02UMA	20524	SN	WX52HSX	20530	SN	WV52HTT
20513	SN	WX51AKY	20519	DC	WK02UMB	20525	BA	WX52KTJ	20531	SN	WV52HVE
20514	SA	WV02EUP	20520	DC	WK02UMC	20526	BA	WX52KTK	20532	SN	WV52HVF
20515	SA	WV02EUR	20521	SN	WV52FAM	20527	BA	WX52KTL	20533	SN	WV52AKY

20534-20549

Volvo B12M · TransBus Paragon · C44FTL · 2003

20534	SN	WX03ZFG	20538	C	CU03AVC	20542	SN	WX53WFA	20546	SN	WX53WGG
20535	SN	WM03BXP	20539	C	CU03AVD	20543	SN	WX53WEW	20547	SN	WX53WGF
20536	DC	WK03EKX	20540	SN	WX53PFJ	20544	SN	WX53WFP	20548	C	CU53AEG
20537	DC	WK03EKW	20541	SN	WX53PFG	20545	SN	WX53WGJ	20549	C	CU53AFZ

20550-20555

Volvo B12M · TransBus Paragon · C44FTL · 2004

20550	C	CU04AYP	20552	LH	WM04NYV	20554	LH	WM04PHK	20555	LH	WM04NZU
20551	C	CU04AYS	20553	LH	WM04NYW					

First now operates four Scania K114s on National Express duties, all from the Bristol depot. Illustrating the type is 23202, YN04YHX, which was seen at Calcot in July 2004. *Dave Heath*

21097	DC	R297AYB	Dennis Javelin GX 12SDA2153	Plaxton Expressliner 2	C49FT	1998
21099	DC	R299AYB	Dennis Javelin GX 12SDA2153	Plaxton Expressliner 2	C49FT	1998
21150	C	S116RKG	Dennis Javelin GX	Plaxton Expressliner 2	C46FT	1999
21151	C	T101XDE	Dennis Javelin GX	Plaxton Expressliner 2	C44FT	1999
21152	C	T102XDE	Dennis Javelin GX	Plaxton Expressliner 2	C44FT	1999
21153	C	T103XDE	Dennis Javelin GX	Plaxton Expressliner 2	C44FT	1999

23201-23204		Scania K114IB	Irizar Century 12.35	C44FT	2004
23201 SN YN04YHW	**23202** SN YNO4YHX	**23203** SN YNO4YHY	**23204** SN YNO4YHZ		

Details of the other vehicles in the First group fleet may be found in the annual First Bus Handbook

FOUR SQUARE

S Riggott, Three Acres, Hoyle Mill Road, Kinsley, Pontefract, WF9 5JB

310	Bradford - Leicester
343	Leeds - Newquay
381	Leeds - Newcastle
693	Leeds - Ty-Mawr

No vehicles are contracted to operate in National Express colours. The vehicles used on the service are selected from the main fleet. Details of the vehicles in this fleet may be found in The Yorkshire Bus Handbook

FREEBIRD

P Dart, Revers Garage, Revers Street, Bury, BL8 1AQ

540	Manchester - London

No vehicles are contracted to operate in National Express colours. The vehicles used on the service are selected from the main fleet.

G & S TRAVEL

G Rimmer, 14 Pysons Road, Ramsgate, CT12 6TS

020	London - Dover
022	London - Ramsgate

No vehicles are contracted to operate in National Express colours. The vehicles used on the service are selected from the main fleet.

GALLOWAY

Galloway European Coachlines Ltd, Denter's Hill, Mendlesham, Stowmarket, IP14 5RR

481	London - Felixstowe
484	London - Clacton-on-Sea
484	London - Walton-on-the-Naze

146	1440PP	DAF DE33WSSB3000	Van Hool Alizée HE	C49FT	1998	Armchair, Brentford, 1999
142	6399PP	DAF DE33WSSB3000	Van Hool T9 Alizée	C49FT	1999	
155	V215EGV	DAF DE33WSSB3000	Van Hool T9 Alizée	C49FT	2000	

Previous registrations

1440PP	R161GNW		6399PP	S53VGV

Details of the other vehicles in this fleet may be found in The Eastern Bus Handbook

GO-NORTH EAST

Go North East Ltd, 117 Queen Street, Bensham, Gateshead, NE8 2UA

304	Weymouth - Liverpool
332	Newcastle - Birmingham
380	Bangor - Liverpool - Newcastle
381	Chester - Leeds - Newcastle
530	Paignton - Newcastle
531	Plymouth - Newcastle
663	Skegness - Newcastle

7062	GSK962	Volvo B10M-62	Plaxton Expressliner 2	C44FT	1997
7074	YSU874	Volvo B10M-62	Plaxton Expressliner 2	C44FT	1997
7075	YSU875	Volvo B10M-62	Plaxton Expressliner 2	C44FT	1997
7076	YSU876	Volvo B10M-62	Plaxton Expressliner 2	C44FT	1997
7077	S977ABR	Volvo B10M-62	Plaxton Expressliner 2	C44FT	1998
7078	S978ABR	Volvo B10M-62	Plaxton Expressliner 2	C44FT	1998
7079	S979ABR	Volvo B10M-62	Plaxton Expressliner 2	C44FT	1998
7080	Y808MFT	Volvo B10M-62	Plaxton Paragon	C49FT	2001
7081	Y781MFT	Volvo B10M-62	Plaxton Paragon	C49FT	2001
7082	Y782MFT	Volvo B10M-62	Plaxton Paragon	C49FT	2001
7083	Y783MFT	Volvo B10M-62	Plaxton Paragon	C49FT	2001
7084	Y784MFT	Volvo B10M-62	Plaxton Paragon	C49FT	2001
7085	Y785MFT	Volvo B10M-62	Plaxton Paragon	C49FT	2001
7086	JCN822	Volvo B12M	Plaxton Paragon Expressliner	C49FT	2002
7087	FCU100	Volvo B12M	Plaxton Paragon Expressliner	C49FT	2002
7088	524FUP	Volvo B12M	Plaxton Paragon Expressliner	C49FT	2003
7089	574CPT	Volvo B12M	Plaxton Paragon Expressliner	C49FT	2003

Previous Registrations:
GSK962   JSK346

Details of the vehicles in this fleet may be found in The Go-Ahead Bus Handbook

Go-North East's contribution to the National Express network uses Plaxton Expressliner 2s like P411MDT of Ambassador, seen here at Coventry. The Expressliner 2 is based on the frame of Plaxton's Première 350 model and features additional items that include driver's partition and fare collection equipment not fitted to the Première. *Mark Doggett*

GOODE'S

K Goode, Farm Garage, Crankhall Lane, Wednesbury, WS10 0ED

420   London - Birmingham

No vehicles are contracted to operate in National Express colours. The vehicles used on the service are selected from the main fleet.

HAYTON

B Hayton, 12 Acorn Close, Burnage, Manchester, M19 2HS

344   Manchester - Newquay
380   Manchester - Llandudno
540   London - Manchester
541   Manchester - London

| 59 | P59XNL | Volvo B10M - 66SE | Plaxton Expressliner 2 | C44FT | 1996 | Durham Travel, 2001 |

Other vehicles used on the services are selected from the main fleet.

IMPACT TRAVEL

T Marley, 1 Leighton Road, Ealing, London, W13 9EL

010   London - Cambridge

No vehicles are contracted to operate in National Express colours. The vehicles used on the service are selected from the main fleet.

INTERNATIONAL COACH LINES

International Coach Lines Ltd, 19 Nursery Road, Thornton Heath, CR7 8RE

020   London - Canterbury
570   London - Blackpool

No vehicles are contracted to operate in National Express colours. The vehicles used on the service are selected from the main fleet.

JOHN PIKE

J Pike, 77 Scott Close, Walworth Industrial Estate, Andover, SP10 5NU

340	Southampton - Birmingham

No vehicles are contracted to operate in National Express colours. The vehicles used on the service are selected from the main fleet.

JONES INTERNATIONAL

M & M Jones, Bron-y-De, Gwynfe, Ffairfach, Llandeilo, Carmarthenshire, SA19 6UY

322	Swansea - Birmingham
672	Swansea - Minehead

No vehicles are contracted to operate in National Express colours. The vehicles used on the service are selected from the main fleet. Details of the vehicles in this fleet may be found in The Welsh Bus Handbook

LEES OF DURHAM

Lees Coaches Ltd, Mill Road Garage, Littleburn Ind Est, Langley Moor, Durham, DH7 8HE

380	Newcastle - Manchester

No vehicles are contracted to operate in National Express colours. The vehicles used on the service are selected from the main fleet. Details of the vehicles in this fleet may be found in The North East Bus Handbook

LOONAT

S M Loonat, 33 Talbot Street, Batley, WF17 5AL

060	Leeds - Liverpool

YS02YYF	Volvo B12M	Plaxton Panther	C49FT	2002
YN52VBG	Volvo B12M	Plaxton Paragon Expressliner	C49FT	2003
YN03WYG	Volvo B12M	Plaxton Paragon Expressliner	C49FT	2003

McNULTY

D McNulty, 41 South Building, 56 Magnet Road, Wembley, HA9 7RQ

450	London - Nottingham
505	London - Newquay
550	London - Liverpool
673	London - Minehead

No vehicles are contracted to operate in National Express colours. The vehicles used on the service are selected from the main fleet.

MOORE'S COACHES

C Moore, 6 Hereford Way, Middlewich, CW10 9GS

538	Manchester Airport - Glasgow

No vehicles are contracted to operate in National Express colours. The vehicles used on the service are selected from the main fleet.

PARK'S OF HAMILTON

Parks of Hamilton (Coach Hirers) Ltd, 20 Bothwell Road, Hamilton, ML3 0AY

534	Glasgow - Hull
537	Glasgow - Lincoln
538	Glasgow - Manchester Airport
590	Glasgow - London
591	Edinburgh - London

HSK641	Volvo B12M	Jonckheere Mistral 50	C49FT	2002
HSK642	Volvo B12M	Jonckheere Mistral 50	C49FT	2002
HSK643	Volvo B12M	Jonckheere Mistral 50	C49FT	2002
HSK644	Volvo B12M	Jonckheere Mistral 50	C49FT	2002

Details of the other vehicles in this fleet may be found in The Scottish Bus Handbook

Park's of Hamilton provide four coaches, all Volvo B12Ms with Jonckheere Mistral 50 bodies, for their National Express duties. Seen pictured in Skipton while working a duty on service 537 from Lincoln to Glasgow is HSK641. *Tony Wilson*

RAPSON'S

Rapsons Coaches Ltd, 1 Seafield Road, Inverness, IV1 1TN

336	Coventry - Glasgow
538	Coventry - Inverness
540	Bolton - London
543	Glasgow - Southampton
588	Inverness - London
590	Glasgow - London

646	V944JST	Volvo B10M-62	Plaxton Première 350	C49FT	2000
648	XIJ602	Volvo B10M-62	Plaxton Paragon	C49FT	2000
650	444VNX	Volvo B10M-62	Plaxton Paragon	C49FT	2000
654	X465XAS	Volvo B10M-62	Plaxton Première 320	C49FT	2001
669	FN04JZR	Volvo B12M	Jonckheere Mistral 50	C49FT	2004
670	FN04JZT	Volvo B12M	Jonckheere Mistral 50	C49FT	2004

Details of the other vehicles in this fleet may be found in The Scottish Bus Handbook

ROADLINER

Roadliner Passenger Transport Ltd, 26 Stourpaine Road, Poole, B17 9AT

035	London - Bournemouth - Swanage

No vehicles are contracted to operate in National Express colours. The vehicles used on the service are selected from the main fleet.

E STOTT & SONS

E Stott & Sons Ltd, Colne Vale Garage, Savile Street, Milnsbridge, Huddersfield, HD3 4PG

541	Bolton - London

No vehicles are contracted to operate in National Express colours. The vehicles used on the service are selected from the main fleet.

SELWYN'S

Selwyns Travel Ltd, Cavendish Farm Road, Weston, Runcorn, WA7 4LU

060	Liverpool - Manchester - Leeds
061	Liverpool - Leeds
303	Birkenhead - Southsea
305	Liverpool - Southend
314	Southport - Cambridge
350	Liverpool - Clacton
383	Wrexham - Edinburgh
420	London - Stafford - Wrexham
422	London - Burnley
440	London - Manchester
533	Wrexham - Glasgow
550	London – Southport
551	London – Liverpool

Latest arrivals with Selwyn's are further Van Hool T9s built on a SB4000 model from VDL Bus, formerly DAF. One of the last with DAF markings is 104, JP03PPZ, which was operating route 305 from Southend when seen. *Dave Heath*

Selwyn's National Express fleet of all DAF-based coaches provides the vehicles for many routes working from north-west England. Coventry bus station is the location for this view of 64, Y469HUA, which was working service 305 to Southend in April 2004. *Mark Doggett*

62	Y467HUA	DAF DE33WSSB3000	Van Hool T9 Alizée	C49FT	2001	
64	Y468HUA	DAF DE33WSSB3000	Van Hool T9 Alizée	C49FT	2001	
68	Y469HUA	DAF DE33WSSB3000	Van Hool T9 Alizée	C49FT	2001	
69	R39GNW	DAF DE33WSSB3000	Van Hool Alizée HE	C49FT	1998	Armchair, Brentford, 2002
74	T174AUA	DAF DE33WSSB3000	Van Hool T9 Alizée	C44FT	1999	
75	Y475HUA	DAF DE33WSSB3000	Van Hool T9 Alizée	C49FT	2001	
76	Y476HUA	DAF DE33WSSB3000	Van Hool T9 Alizée	C49FT	2001	
77	S428JUA	DAF DE33WSSB3000	Ikarus Blue Danube 396	C49FT	1999	Windmill, Copford, 2001
79	W226CDN	DAF DE33WSSB3000	Ikarus Blue Danube 396	C49FT	2000	Airlinks, Heathrow, 2001
90	YJ51EKX	DAF DE33WSSB3000	Van Hool T9 Alizée	C49FT	2002	
91	YJ51EKY	DAF DE33WSSB3000	Van Hool T9 Alizée	C49FT	2002	
92	YJ51EKZ	DAF DE33WSSB3000	Van Hool T9 Alizée	C49FT	2002	
93	TJI6925	DAF DE33WSSB3000	Van Hool T9 Alizée	C49FT	1999	Peter Carol, Bristol, 2002
94	R36GNW	DAF DE33WSSB3000	Van Hool Alizée HE	C49FT	1998	Armchair, Brentford, 2002
95	R59GNW	DAF DE33WSSB3000	Van Hool Alizée HE	C49FT	1998	Armchair, Brentford, 2002
96	R61GNW	DAF DE33WSSB3000	Van Hool Alizée HE	C49FT	1998	Arriva Bus & Coach, 2002
97	R62GNW	DAF DE33WSSB3000	Van Hool Alizée HE	C49FT	1998	Armchair, Brentford, 2002
98	T58AUA	DAF DE33WSSB3000	Van Hool T9 Alizée	C49FT	1999	Fishwick, Leyland, 2002
101	352STG	DAF DE33WSSB3000	Van Hool Alizée HE	C49FT	1996	Reading Buses, 2002
102	S426JUA	DAF DE33WSSB3000	Ikarus Blue Danube 396	C49FT	1998	Arriva Bus & Coach, 2002
103	YJ03PPY	DAF DE40XSSB4000	Van Hool T9 Alizée	C49FT	2003	
104	YJ03PPZ	DAF DE40XSSB4000	Van Hool T9 Alizée	C49FT	2003	
105	YJ53VDN	DAF DE40XSSB4000	Van Hool T9 Alizée	C49FT	2003	
106	YJ53VDO	DAF DE40XSSB4000	Van Hool T9 Alizée	C49FT	2003	
107	YJ04BYH	VDL Bus SB4000	Van Hool T9 Alizée	C49FT	2004	
108	YJ04BYK	VDL Bus SB4000	Van Hool T9 Alizée	C49FT	2004	
		VDL Bus SB4000	Van Hool T9 Alizée	C49FT	2004	
		VDL Bus SB4000	Van Hool T9 Alizée	C49FT	On order	
		VDL Bus SB4000	Van Hool T9 Alizée	C49FT	On order	
		VDL Bus SB4000	Van Hool T9 Alizée	C49FT	On order	

Acquired from the Airlinks fleet by Selwyn's in 2001 and numbered 79, W226CDN is a DAF SB3000 with Ikarus Blue Danube 396 bodywork. It is seen at Calcot, some 10km to the west of Reading. It is one of only three Ikarus coaches now in National Express colours. *Dave Heath*

Previous registration

352STG	N74FWU	R39GNW	R39GNW, 98D70419
TJI6925	T118AUA		

Details of the other vehicles in this fleet may be found in The North West Bus Handbook

SILVERDALE

Silverdale London Ltd, 3 Radford Estate, Old Oak Lane, London, NW10 6UA

010	London - Cambridge
040	London - Bristol
420	London - Birmingham

No vehicles are contracted to operate in National Express colours. The vehicles used on the service are selected from the main fleet.

STAGECOACH

020	London - Dover	SE
021	London - Dover	SE
022	London - Ramsgate	SE
023	London - Bexhill	NW
024	London - Hastings	SE
230	Gatwick - Mansfield	EM (to 9/04)
310	Bradford - Leicester	SM
320	Birmingham - Bradford	SM
320	Oxford - Bradford	SM
324	Paignton - Bradford	SM
325	Manchester - Birmingham	NW
333	Blackpool - Bournemouth	NW
337	Brixham - Rugby	SM
341	Burnley - Birmingham - Paignton	NW
350	Liverpool - Cambridge	EM
412	London - Worcester	CG (to 9/04)
412	London - Gloucester	CG (to 9/04)
448	London - Grimsby	EA
448	London - Lincoln	EA
448	London - Peterborough	EA
449	London - Mablethorpe	EA

Many of Stagecoach's early Expressliners were displaced in the late 1990s with Jonckheere Mistral 50 coaches. Weymouth is the location for this view of 52623, S903CCD, which was leaving the town for the north-west coastal resort of Blackpool. *Tony Wilson*

Stagecoach operates National Express services from several parts of the country, and allocates its coaches, liveried for the contracts, accordingly. Pictured near Hyde Park is 52453, R553JDF, which currently operates from the City of Preston. *Tony Wilson*

450	Liverpool - Mansfield	EM
455	London - Northampton	SM (to 9/04)
455	London - Rugby	SM
460	London - Stratford-upon-Avon	SM
460	London - Coventry	SM
535	Kettering - Dundee	ES
540	London - Burnley	NW
540	London - Bury	NW
561	London - Bradford	SM
570	London - Blackpool	NW
570	London - Whitehaven	NW
590	London - Aberdeen	NW

Stagecoach vehicles for National Express:

52268	LL	M165SCK	Volvo B10M-62	Plaxton Expressliner 2	C46FT	1994
52308	RU	N618USS	Volvo B10M-62	Plaxton Expressliner 2	C44FT	1995
52382	PH	P622ESO	Volvo B10M-62	Plaxton Expressliner 2	C44FT	1997
52387	PH	P627ESO	Volvo B10M-62	Plaxton Expressliner 2	C44FT	1997

52434-52439 Volvo B10M-62 Plaxton Expressliner 2 C49FT 1997

| 52434 | RU | R34AKV | 52436 | RU | R36AKV | 52438 | RU | R38AKV | 52439 | RU | R39AKV |
| 52435 | RU | R35AKV | 52437 | RU | R37AKV | | | | | | |

52444-52447 Volvo B10M-62 Plaxton Expressliner 2 C49FT* 1997 *seating varies

| 52444 | RU | R454FCE | 52445 | PE | R455FCE | 52446 | PE | R456FCE | 52447 | RU | R453FCE |

52450-52454 Volvo B10M-62 Plaxton Expressliner 2 C49FT* 1997 *seating varies

| 52450 | RU | R550JDF | 52452 | LL | R552JDF | 52453 | PR | R553JDF | 52454 | PR | R554JDF |
| 52451 | PR | R551JDF | | | | | | | | | |

Cheltenham is the western termus for route 412. In September 2004, Stagecoach were replaced on the service by vehicles from First, thus leading to the re-allocation of several coaches. *Dave Heath*

52490	PR	R120VFR	Volvo B10M-62	Jonckheere Mistral 50	C44FT	1998	
52493	MD	R663TKU	Volvo B10M-62	Plaxton Expressliner 2	C44FT	1997	
52494	MD	R664TKU	Volvo B10M-62	Plaxton Expressliner 2	C44FT	1997	
52601	MD	S173SVK	Volvo B10M-62	Jonckheere Mistral 50	C44FT	1998	
52602	MD	S174SVK	Volvo B10M-62	Jonckheere Mistral 50	C44FT	1998	
52603	LL	S133KRM	Volvo B10M-62	Jonckheere Mistral 50	C44FT	1998	
52604	LL	S134KRM	Volvo B10M-62	Jonckheere Mistral 50	C44FT	1998	
52615	PR	S905JHG	Volvo B10M-62	Jonckheere Mistral 50	C44FT	1998	
52616	PR	S906JHG	Volvo B10M-62	Jonckheere Mistral 50	C44FT	1998	

52617-52620   Volvo B10M-62   Jonckheere Mistral 50   C49FT   1988

52617	PE	S457BCE	52618	PE	S458BCE	52619	PE	S459BCE	52620	PE	S460BCE

52621	DO	S901CCD	Volvo B10M-62	Jonckheere Mistral 50	C49FT	1998	
52622	PR	S902CCD	Volvo B10M-62	Jonckheere Mistral 50	C46FT	1998	
52623	PR	S903CCD	Volvo B10M-62	Jonckheere Mistral 50	C46FT	1998	
52635	MD	S665SDT	Volvo B10M-62	Jonckheere Mistral 50	C44FT	1998	

52641-52649   Volvo B10M-62   Jonckheere Mistral 50   C44FT*   1999   *seating varies

52641	RU	T661OBD	52643	RU	T663OBD	52645	MD	KSU462	52648	MD	T668XTV
52642	RU	T662OBD	52644	MD	KSU461	52647	PH	T667XTV	52649	MD	T669XTV

52654-52659   Volvo B10M-62   Jonckheere Mistral 50   C49FT   1999

52654	TH	V904DPN	52656	TH	V906DPN	52658	DO	V908DDY	52659	TH	V909DDY
52655	TH	V905DPN	52657	DO	V907DDY						

53001-53010   Volvo B12M   Plaxton Paragon Expressliner   C46FT   2002

53001	DO	GU52WSX	53004	DO	GU52WTA	53007	DO	GU52WTE	53009	DO	GU52WTG
53002	DO	GU52WSY	53005	DO	GU52WTC	53008	DO	GU52WTF	53010	DO	GU52WTJ
53003	DO	GU52WSZ	53006	DO	GU52WTD						

Purchased for the London to Dover service, the 2002 delivery of Plaxton Paragon Expressliners included nearside destination displays as shown on 53006, GU52WTD. This batch also comprised the first centre-engined Volvo B12M coaches for the fleet. *Dave Heath*

53011-53022   Volvo B12M   Plaxton Paragon Expressliner C46FT*   2003   *seating varies

53011	MD	YN03WNA	53014	CT	VU03VVY	53017	CT	VU03VVW	53020	LL	PX03KCV
53012	CT	VU03VVW	53015	CT	VU03VVZ	53018	PR	PX03KCN	53021	LL	PX03KCY
53013	CT	VU03VVX	53016	CT	VU03VWA	53019	PR	PX03KCU	53022	MD	YV03TZN

Previous registrations

| S173SVK | 1JVK | | | | |
| S174SVK | 2JVK | | TSU639 | R456FCE | |

Details of the other vehicles in the Stagecoach fleet, along with allocation code details may be found in the annual Stagecoach Bus Handbook.

TRAVELLERS' CHOICE

Shaw Hadwin (John Shaw & Sons) Ltd, The Coach and Travel Centre, Scotland Road, Carnforth, LA5 9BQ

570   Blackpool - London

No vehicles are contracted to operate in National Express colours. The vehicles used on the service are selected from the main fleet. Details of the vehicles in this fleet may be found in The North West Bus Handbook

TELLINGS-GOLDEN MILLER

Tellings-Golden Miller Ltd, The Old Tram Garage, Stanley Road, Twickenham, TW2 5NS

010	London - Cambridge
025	London - Worthing
030	London - Portsmouth
031	London - Portsmouth
032	London - Portsmouth
032	London - Southampton
300	Southsea - Bristol
310	Southsea - Bradford

R10TGM	Volvo B10M-62	Van Hool T9 Alizèe	C48FT	1998	
R20TGM	Volvo B10M-62	Van Hool T9 Alizèe	C48FT	1998	
R584GDX	Volvo B10M-62	Plaxton Excalibur	C49FT	1998	Burtons, Haverhill, 2003
R595GDX	Volvo B10M-62	Plaxton Excalibur	C49FT	1998	Burtons, Haverhill, 2003
KP51SYF	Volvo B10M-62	Plaxton Panther	C49FT	2002	
KP51UEV	Volvo B10M-62	Plaxton Panther	C49FT	2002	
KP51UEW	Volvo B10M-62	Plaxton Panther	C49FT	2002	
KP51UEX	Volvo B10M-62	Plaxton Panther	C49FT	2002	
KP51UEY	Volvo B10M-62	Plaxton Panther	C49FT	2002	
KP51UEZ	Volvo B10M-62	Plaxton Panther	C49FT	2002	
KU02YUF	Volvo B12M	Plaxton Paragon	C49FT	2002	
KU02YUG	Volvo B12M	Plaxton Paragon	C49FT	2002	
LB52UYK	Volvo B12M	Plaxton Paragon	C49FT	2003	
KX04HSJ	Volvo B12M	TransBus Paragon	C49FT	2004	

Details of the other vehicles in this fleet may be found in the London Bus Handbook

Joining the Tellings fleet in 2003, LB52UYK is one of four B12M coaches. Under TransBus ownership the Plaxton name continued until early 2003. During the summer of 2004, Plaxton management along with a private equity company purchased this part of TransBus and re-established the Plaxton name once again.
Dave Heath

TRATHENS

Trathens Travel Services Ltd, Walkham Park, Burrington Way, Plymouth, PL5 3LS

421	London - Blackpool
500	London - Penzance
501	London - Plymouth - Brixham
504	London - Penzance
538	Manchester Airport - Aberdeen
540	London - Rochdale/Burnley
570	London - Blackpool
592	London - Aberdeen

498	LSK498	Volvo B12T	Van Hool Astrobel	C57/14CT	1998
499	LSK499	Volvo B12T	Van Hool Astrobel	C57/14CT	1998
503	LSK503	Volvo B12M	Jonckheere Mistral 50	C49FT	2004
504	LSK504	Volvo B12M	Jonckheere Mistral 50	C49FT	2004
505	LSK505	Volvo B12M	Jonckheere Mistral 50	C49FT	2004
506	LSK506	Volvo B12M	Jonckheere Mistral 50	C49FT	2004
507	LSK507	Volvo B12M	Jonckheere Mistral 50	C49FT	2004
508	LSK508	Volvo B12M	Jonckheere Mistral 50	C49FT	2004
511	LSK511	Volvo B12T	Van Hool Astrobel	C57/14CT	1997
512	LSK512	Volvo B12T	Van Hool Astrobel	C57/14CT	1997
513	YN51XMW	Neoplan Skyliner N122/3	Neoplan	C57/14FT	2001
514	YN51XMX	Neoplan Skyliner N122/3	Neoplan	C57/14FT	2002
515	YN51XMK	Neoplan Skyliner N122/3	Neoplan	C57/14FT	2002
516	YN51XML	Neoplan Skyliner N122/3	Neoplan	C57/14FT	2002

Seen calling into London Heathrow is LSK507 from the Trathens Fleet. Six new Jonckheere Mistral 50 arrived in 2004, replacing similar examples new in 2001. These can be found on the extensive network that Trathens operate for National Express.Trathens are owned by Park's of Hamilton and vehicles are often transferred between the two operations. *Dave Heath*

Some forty years ago, Standerwick operated services between London and Lancashire using double-deck coaches with air-suspension. These were the latest model of the Leyland Atlantean and carried the 'Gay Hostess' branding. Now plying the same service for National Express, Trathens operates Neoplan Skyliners on the route. Seen heading out of London for Burnley is 518, YN51XNC. *Tony Wilson*

517	YN51XMZ	Neoplan Skyliner N122/3	Neoplan	C57/14FT	2002	
518	YN51XNC	Neoplan Skyliner N122/3	Neoplan	C57/14FT	2002	
519	YN51XND	Neoplan Skyliner N122/3	Neoplan	C57/14FT	2002	
520	YN51XNE	Neoplan Skyliner N122/3	Neoplan	C57/14FT	2002	
521	YN51XMH	Neoplan Skyliner N122/3	Neoplan	C57/14FT	2002	
522	YN51XMJ	Neoplan Skyliner N122/3	Neoplan	C57/14FT	2002	
523	YN51XMU	Neoplan Skyliner N122/3	Neoplan	C57/14FT	2001	
524	YN51XMV	Neoplan Skyliner N122/3	Neoplan	C57/14FT	2001	
651	HSK651	Volvo B12M	Jonckheere Mistral 50	C49FT	2003	Parks of Hamilton, 2004
652	HSK652	Volvo B12M	Jonckheere Mistral 50	C49FT	2003	Parks of Hamilton, 2004
653	HSK653	Volvo B12M	Jonckheere Mistral 50	C49FT	2003	Parks of Hamilton, 2004

Previous registrations

| LSK498 | R261OHJ | | LSK511 | P926KYC |
| LSK499 | R264OHJ | | LSK512 | P927KYC |

Details of the other vehicles in this fleet may be found in The South West Bus Handbook.

TRAVEL DUNDEE

Tayside Public Transport Company Ltd, 44-48 East Dock Street, Dundee, DD1 3JS

| 592 | | Dundee - London |

No vehicles are contracted to operate in National Express colours. The vehicles used on the service are selected from the main fleet. Details of the vehicles in this fleet may be found in The Scottish Bus Handbook

TRENT

Trent Motor Traction Co. Ltd, 88A Mansfield Road, Heanor, Derbyshire, DE75 7BG

326	Nottingham - Newcastle
440	London - Derby
450	London - Mansfield
450	London - Retford

9	V209JAL	Volvo B10M-62	Plaxton Expressliner 2	C49FT	1999
10	V210JAL	Volvo B10M-62	Plaxton Expressliner 2	C49FT	1999
11	V211JAL	Volvo B10M-62	Plaxton Expressliner 2	C49FT	1999
12	V212JAL	Volvo B10M-62	Plaxton Expressliner 2	C49FT	1999
13	X913ERA	Volvo B10M-62	Plaxton Expressliner 2	C49FT	2000
14	X914ERA	Volvo B10M-62	Plaxton Expressliner 2	C49FT	2000
15	X915ERA	Volvo B10M-62	Plaxton Expressliner 2	C49FT	2000

Details of the other vehicles in this fleet may be found in The East Midland Bus Handbook

Trent's contribution to the National Express network uses Plaxton Expressliner 2s including number 15, X915ERA, seen here near Hyde Park. All seven of the Expressliners in the fleet were replaced in consecutive years. *Tony Wilson*

TRURONIAN

Truronian Ltd, 24 Lemon Street, Truro, Cornwall, TR1 2LS

344   Newquay - Manchester

No vehicles are contracted to operate in National Express colours. The vehicles used on the service are selected from the main fleet. Details of the vehicles in this fleet may be found in The South West Bus Handbook

TURNER'S COACHWAYS

Turner's Coachways (Bristol) Ltd, 59 Days Road, St Phillips, Bristol, BS2 0QS

040   London - Bristol

No vehicles are contracted to operate in National Express colours. The vehicles used on the service are selected from the main fleet. Details of the vehicles in this fleet may be found in The South West Bus Handbook

TURNER'S TOURS

A R & ME Turner & S L & P C Gilson, 1 Fore Street, Chumleigh, Devon, EX18 7BR

341   Birmingham - Exeter

No vehicles are contracted to operate in National Express colours. The vehicles used on the service are selected from the main fleet.

T W H

TWH Travel Ltd, The Gas Works, 709 Old Kent Road, London, SE15 1JJ

040   London - Bristol

No vehicles are contracted to operate in National Express colours. The vehicles used on the service are selected from the main fleet. Details of the vehicles in this fleet may be found in The London Bus Handbook

WILTS & DORSET

Wilts & Dorset Bus Co Ltd, Towngate House, 2-8 Parkstone Road, Poole, BH15 2PR

| 032 | London - Salisbury |
| 033 | London - Yeovil |

3216	T216REL	DAF DE33WSSB3000	Plaxton Prima	C49FT	1999
3217	T217REL	DAF DE33WSSB3000	Plaxton Prima	C49FT	1999
3218	T218REL	DAF DE33WSSB3000	Plaxton Prima	C49FT	1999

Details of the other vehicles in this fleet may be found in The Go-Ahead Bus Handbook

The Prima body from Plaxton was an adaptation of the Première for rear-engined chassis, such as the Volvo B7R and DAF SB3000. Wilts & Dorset operates three of the latter, represented by 3217, T217REL.
Dave Heath

YARDLEY'S

Yardley's Travel Ltd, 68-72 Berkeley Road East, Hay Mills, Birmingham, B25 8NP

310	Coventry - Leeds
310	Birmingham - Leeds
545	Birmingham - Llandudno
661	Birmingham - Skegness

No vehicles are contracted to operate in National Express colours. The vehicles used on the service are selected from the main fleet.

YEOMANS

Yeomans Canyon Travel Ltd, 21-3 Three Elms Trading Estate, Hereford, HR4 9PU

413   Hereford - London

64	W634MKY	Volvo B10M-62	Plaxton Expressliner 2	C44FT	2000
22	YP52CTV	Scania K114IB4	Van Hool T9 Alizée	C49FT	2002
01	YR52VEO	Scania K114IB4	Van Hool T9 Alizée	C49FT	2002

Details of the other vehicles in this fleet may be found in The West Midlands Bus Handbook

euroLines operations from the UK are listed in the table on page 61. Here a euroLines coach from France is seen at London Victoria. The model is a Setra S315 Comfortclass model GT-HD *Philip Ratcliffe*

YORKSHIRE TRACTION

The Yorkshire Traction Co. Ltd, Upper Sheffield Road, Barnsley, S70 4PP

061	Leeds - Liverpool
070	Sheffield - Leeds
070	Sheffield - Bradford
310	Bradford - Poole
312	Barnsley - Blackpool
335	Halifax - Poole
351	Blackpool - Sheffield
465	London - Huddersfield
560	Barnsley - London
564	London - Halifax

42	6078HE	DAF DE33WSSB3000	Van Hool Alizée H	C44FT	1998	Arriva Yorkshire, 2000
45	V345EKW	Mercedes-Benz O404-15R	Hispano Vita	C44FT	2000	
47	YHE91	Volvo B10M-62	Plaxton Première 350	C49FT	1999	Parks of Hamilton, 2001
48	2408HE	Volvo B10M-62	Plaxton Première 350	C49FT	1999	Parks of Hamilton, 2001
49	YTC49	Volvo B10M-62	Plaxton Première 350	C49FT	1999	Parks of Hamilton, 2001
61	6087HE	Volvo B10M-62	Plaxton Expressliner 2	C44FT	1998	
62	OHE50	Volvo B10M-62	Plaxton Expressliner 2	C44FT	1998	
63	2542HE	Volvo B10M-62	Plaxton Expressliner 2	C44FT	1998	
64	YTC856	Volvo B10M-62	Plaxton Expressliner 2	C44FT	1999	
65	1619HE	Volvo B10M-62	Plaxton Expressliner 2	C44FT	1999	
66	1737HE	Volvo B10M-62	Plaxton Paragon	C49FT	2001	
67	Y967PHL	Volvo B10M-62	Plaxton Paragon	C49FT	2001	

Seen passing through Chesterfield, Yorkshire Traction's 64, YTC856, is one of six Plaxton Expressliner 2s in the fleet. The coach was operating the Barnsley to London service, one of its regular routes. *Tony Wilson*

Four coaches for National Express work joined the Yorkshire Traction fleet in 2004. These are Volvo B12Ms with Plaxton Paragon Expressliner bodies. *Tony Wilson*

68	YS02YXR	Volvo B12M	Plaxton Paragon	C49FT	2002
69	YS02YXT	Volvo B12M	Plaxton Paragon	C49FT	2002
70	YU04YAG	Volvo B12B	Plaxton Paragon Expressliner	C49FT	2004
71	YU04YAH	Volvo B12B	Plaxton Paragon Expressliner	C49FT	2004
72	YU04YBG	Volvo B12B	Plaxton Paragon Expressliner	C49FT	2004
73	YU04YBF	Volvo B12B	Plaxton Paragon Expressliner	C49FT	2004
81	4195HE	Scania K113CRB	Van Hool Alizée HE	C46FT	1996
82	1533HE	Scania K113CRB	Van Hool Alizée HE	C46FT	1996

Previous Registrations:

1533HE	N281CAK	6078HE	R32SYB
1619HE	S365VKW	6087HE	R761XWG
1737HE	Y966PHL	OHE50	R762XWG
2408HE	T871RGA	YHE91	T870RGA
2542HE	R763XWG	YTC49	T872RGA
4195HE	M281CAK	YTC856	S364VKW

Details of the other vehicles in this fleet may be found in The Yorkshire Bus Handbook

ZAK'S

K P Fazakarley, 319 Shady Lane, Great Barr, Birmingham, B44 9ER

389	Birmingham - Blackpool
460	Coventry - Warwick - London

No vehicles are contracted to operate in National Express colours. The vehicles used on the service are selected from the main fleet. Details of the vehicles in this fleet may be found in The West Midlands Bus Handbook

Index to National Express routes

euroLines Services from the UK

120-4/6	London - Amiens - Paris
121/221	London - Disneyland - Paris
121/3	London - Paris - Portugal
125	Amsterdam - Brussels - Paris
127/8	London - Bilbao - Oviedo
129	London - Corunna
130-3	London - Geneva
130/1	London - Clermont Ferrand
131/2	London - Lyon - Chamonix
132/4	London - Marseilles - Nice
132/5	London - Avignon - Narbonne
137	London - Strasbourg - Zurich
140-4	London - Amsterdam
168	London - Arnhem
142(274)	London - Amsterdam - Berlin
140(274)	London - Amsterdam - Hamburg
146	London - Copenhagen
147	London - Alborg/Hirtshals
151	London - Milan - Rome
152-5	London - Genoa - Siena - Venice
160/1	London - Barcelona - Murcia
162/3/5	London - Frankfurt - Munich
164	London - Cologne - Dresden
167/8	London - Lille - Brussels
169	London - Brussels - Luxembourg
170-4	London - Eindhoven - northern Germany
180/1	London - Madrid - Seville - Algeciras
182	London - Madrid
183/5	London - Bordeaux - Lourdes - San Sebastian - Saragossa
184/6/9	London - Toulouse - Andorra
187	London - Nantes - La Rochelle
188	London - Arcachon - Bayonne
190/1/6	London - Salzburg - Vienna
190	London - Bratislava - Kosice
191	London - Vienna - Budapest
192	London - Prague - Ostrava
193	London - Warsaw
194	London - Cracow
195	London - Olsztyn
162(498)	London - Frankfurt - Belgrade
162(418)	London - Frankfurt - Sarajevo
163(497)	London - Zagreb
163(409)	London - Split
163(250)	London - Frankfurt - Bucharest
284/5	London - Sweden
876	Holyhead - Birmingham - Brussels - Frankfurt - Munich

The brand name euroLines unites more than thirty independent coach companies, thus operating Europe's largest regular coach network. This network connects over 500 destinations, covering the whole of the continent as well as Morocco. euroLines allows travelling from Sicily to Helsinki and from Casablanca to Moscow. Operated by the Spanish operator Linesur, this Irizar Century-bodied Volvo waits time in Brussels.
Philip Ratcliffe

Vehicle Index

Reg	Operator	Reg	Operator	Reg	Operator	Reg	Operator
352STG	Selwyns	HSK642	Parks	N21ARC	National Express	P246AAP	National Express
4195HE	Yorkshire Traction	HSK643	Parks	N40SLK	National Express	P247AAP	National Express
444VNX	Rapsons	HSK644	Parks	N50SLK	National Express	P248AAP	National Express
524FUP	Go North East	JCN822	Go North East	N60SLK	National Express	P249AAP	National Express
574CPT	Go North East	K127OCT	Chenery	N70SLK	National Express	P250AAP	National Express
662NKR	Arriva Midlands	KP51SYF	Tellings	N80SLK	National Express	P251AAP	National Express
1440PP	Galloway	KP51UEV	Tellings	N90SLK	National Express	P313CVE	National Express
1533HE	Yorkshire Traction	KP51UEW	Tellings	N112UHP	National Express	P314CVE	National Express
1619HE	Yorkshire Traction	KP51UEX	Tellings	N113UHP	National Express	P315DVE	National Express
1737HE	Yorkshire Traction	KP51UEY	Tellings	N114UHP	National Express	P333SAS	National Express
2408HE	Yorkshire Traction	KP51UEZ	Tellings	N115UHP	National Express	P411MDT	Ambassador
2542HE	Yorkshire Traction	KSU461	Stagecoach	N116UHP	National Express	P412MDT	Ambassador
3277KH	East Yorkshire	KSU462	Stagecoach	N117UHP	National Express	P444SAS	National Express
6078HE	Yorkshire Traction	KU02YUF	Tellings	N118UHP	National Express	P521PRL	First
6087HE	Yorkshire Traction	KU02YUG	Tellings	N119UHP	National Express	P622ESO	Stagecoach
6399PP	Galloway	KX04HSJ	Tellings	N120UHP	National Express	P627ESO	Stagecoach
A3XCL	Excelsior	L50SAS	National Express	N121UHP	National Express	P803BLJ	Ambassador
A7XCL	Excelsior	LB52UYK	Tellings	N122UHP	National Express	P804BLJ	First
A8FTG	Dunn-Line	LK53KVO	National Express	N123UHP	National Express	PX03KCN	Stagecoach
A8XCL	Excelsior	LK53KVP	National Express	N309VAV	National Express	PX03KCU	Stagecoach
A9XCL	Excelsior	LK53KVR	National Express	N310VAV	National Express	PX03KCV	Stagecoach
BC51NAT	Bruces	LK53KVT	National Express	N311VAV	National Express	PX03KCY	Stagecoach
CN04NFD	Bebb	LK53KVU	National Express	N312VAV	National Express	R10TGM	Tellings
CN04NFE	Bebb	LK53KVV	National Express	N825DKU	National Express	R20TGM	Tellings
CN04NFF	Bebb	LK53KVW	National Express	N826DKU	National Express	R34AKV	Stagecoach
CN04NFG	Bebb	LK53KVX	National Express	N827DKU	National Express	R35AKV	Stagecoach
CN51XNU	Bebb	LK53KVY	National Express	N828DKU	National Express	R36AKV	Stagecoach
CN51XNV	Bebb	LK53KVZ	National Express	N829DKU	National Express	R36GNW	Selwyns
CN51XNW	Bebb	LK53KWA	National Express	NK51ORJ	Dunn Line	R37AKV	Stagecoach
CN51XNX	Bebb	LK53KWB	National Express	NK51ORN	Dunn Line	R38AKV	Stagecoach
CN51XNY	Bebb	LK53KWD	National Express	NK51ORO	Dunn Line	R39AKV	Stagecoach
CN51XNZ	Bebb	LK53KWE	National Express	NL52XZV	Arriva North East	R39AWO	Chenery
CN53NWB	Bebb	LK53KWF	National Express	NL52XZW	Arriva North East	R39GNW	Selwyns
CN53NWC	Bebb	LK53KXA	National Express	NL52XZX	Arriva North East	R59GNW	Selwyns
CU03AVC	First	LK53KXB	National Express	NL52XZY	Arriva North East	R61GNW	Selwyns
CU03AVD	First	LSK498	Trathens	OHE50	Yorkshire Traction	R62GNW	Selwyns
CU04AYP	First	LSK499	Trathens	P30SAS	National Express	R85DVF	Ambassador
CU04AYS	First	LSK500	Trathens	P50SAS	National Express	R91GTM	National Express
CU53AEG	First	LSK502	Trathens	P70SAS	National Express	R92GTM	National Express
CU53AFZ	First	LSK503	Trathens	P80SAS	National Express	R100SPK	National Express
ECZ9138	Dunn Line	LSK504	Trathens	P90SAS	National Express	R120VFR	Stagecoach
ECZ9139	Dunn Line	LSK505	Trathens	P111SAS	National Express	R200SPK	National Express
FA04LJK	Dunn-Line	LSK506	Trathens	P201RWR	Arriva Midlands	R297AYB	First
FCU190	Go North East	LSK507	Trathens	P205RWR	Arriva Midlands	R300SPK	National Express
FN03DYA	Excelsior	LSK508	Trathens	P222SAS	National Express	R303EEX	Chenery
FN03DYB	Excelsior	LSK511	Trathens	P226AAP	National Express	R304EEX	Chenery
FN04JZR	Rapsons	LSK512	Trathens	P227AAP	National Express	R304JAF	First
FN04JZT	Rapsons	M58LBB	Go North East	P228AAP	National Express	R305JAF	First
FN52HRG	Ambassador	M59LBB	Go North East	P229AAP	National Express	R307JAF	First
FN52HRM	Ambassador	M165SCK	Stagecoach	P230AAP	National Express	R308JAF	First
GSK962	Go North East	M301BAV	National Express	P231AAP	National Express	R309JAF	First
GU52WSX	Stagecoach	M302BAV	National Express	P232AAP	National Express	R310JAF	First
GU52WSY	Stagecoach	M303BAV	National Express	P233AAP	National Express	R326NRU	Bournemouth
GU52WSZ	Stagecoach	M304BAV	National Express	P234AAP	National Express	R327NRU	Bournemouth
GU52WTA	Stagecoach	M305BAV	National Express	P234BFJ	First	R329NRU	Bournemouth
GU52WTC	Stagecoach	M306BAV	National Express	P235AAP	National Express	R338NEV	Bournemouth
GU52WTD	Stagecoach	M307BAV	National Express	P236AAP	National Express	R354NRU	Bournemouth
GU52WTE	Stagecoach	M308BAV	National Express	P236CTA	First	R355NRU	Bournemouth
GU52WTF	Stagecoach	M716KPD	National Express	P237AAP	National Express	R400SPK	National Express
GU52WTG	Stagecoach	M721KPD	National Express	P238AAP	National Express	R453FCE	Stagecoach
GU52WTJ	Stagecoach	M722KPD	National Express	P239AAP	National Express	R454FCE	Stagecoach
H395SYG	National Express	M723KPD	National Express	P240AAP	National Express	R455FCE	Stagecoach
H396SYG	National Express	M724KPD	National Express	P241AAP	National Express	R500SPK	National Express
H843UUA	National Express	M725KPD	National Express	P242AAP	National Express	R550JDF	Stagecoach
HF53OBG	Bournemouth	M743KJU	Ambassador	P243AAP	National Express	R551JDF	Stagecoach
HF53QBH	Bournemouth	M765CWS	First	P244AAP	National Express	R551JDF	Stagecoach
HSK641	Parks			P245AAP	National Express	R552JDF	Stagecoach

During 2002, Dunn-Line acquired the operations of Flight's of Birmingham and Durham Travel, and the company now operates an extensive network of routes for National Express. The 2003 vehicle intake comprised Volvo B10Ms with Plaxton Excalibur bodywork, represented by this view of W385PRC's arrival at London. *Tony Wilson*

R554JDF	Stagecoach	S324VNM	National Express	T73WWV	National Express	T661OBD	Stagecoach
R584GDX	Tellings	S364OOB	Dunn-Line	T74WWV	National Express	T662OBD	Stagecoach
R595GDX	Tellings	S365OOB	Dunn-Line	T75WWV	National Express	T663OBD	Stagecoach
R663TKU	Stagecoach	S426JUA	Selwyns	T76WWV	National Express	T667XTV	Stagecoach
R664TKU	Stagecoach	S428JUA	Selwyns	T101XDE	First	T668XTV	Stagecoach
R813HWS	First	S457BCE	Stagecoach	T102XDE	First	T669XTV	Stagecoach
R814HWS	First	S458BCE	Stagecoach	T103XDE	First	T868RGA	First
R943LHT	First	S459BCE	Stagecoach	T119AVA	Arriva Midlands	T869RGA	First
S26DTS	Dunn Line	S460BCE	Stagecoach	T174AUA	Selwyns	T948UEU	First
S27DTS	Dunn Line	S665SDT	Stagecoach	T174FUM	Birmingham CC	T949JUG	Birmingham CC
S104JGB	First	S901CDD	Stagecoach	T178FUM	Birmingham CC	TJI6925	Selwyns
S105JGB	First	S902CCD	Stagecoach	T205AUA	National Express	TSU639	Stagecoach
S116RKG	First	S903CCD	Stagecoach	T206AUA	National Express		
S133KRM	Stagecoach	S905JHG	Stagecoach	T207AUA	National Express		
S134KRM	Stagecoach	S906JHG	Stagecoach	T208AUA	National Express		
S173SVK	Stagecoach	S930ATO	National Express	T209AUA	National Express		
S174SVK	Stagecoach	S977ABR	Go North East	T209XVO	Arriva Midlands		
S295WOA	Dunn-Line	S978ABR	Go North East	T210AUA	National Express		
S296WOA	Dunn-Line	S979ABR	Go North East	T211AUA	National Express		
S297WOA	Dunn-Line	T36EUA	Birmingham CC	T216REL	Wilts & Dorset		
S298WOA	Dunn-Line	T37EUA	Birmingham CC	T217REL	Wilts & Dorset		
S311SCV	First	T38EUA	Birmingham CC	T218REL	Wilts & Dorset		
S312SCV	First	T39CNN	Dunn Line	T310AHY	First		
S313SCV	First	T58AUA	Selwyns	T316KCV	First		
S320VNM	National Express	T64BHY	First	T325APP	National Express		
S322VNM	National Express	T71WWV	National Express	T330AFX	Bournemouth		
S323VNM	National Express	T72WWV	National Express	T331AFX	Bournemouth		

Reg	Operator	Reg	Operator	Reg	Operator	Reg	Operator
V10NAT	Bruces	WK02UMB	First	Y97HTX	Bebb	YN03WNA	Stagecoach
V141EJR	Arriva North East	WK02UMC	First	Y301HUA	National Express	YN03WYG	Loonat
V142EJR	Arriva North East	WK03EKW	First	Y302HUA	National Express	YN04GKL	National Express
V209JAL	Trent	WK03EKX	First	Y303HUA	National Express	YN04GKP	National Express
V210JAL	Trent	WK52SVU	First	Y304HUA	National Express	YN04GKU	National Express
V211JAL	Trent	WK52SVV	First	Y307HUA	National Express	YN04GKV	National Express
V212JAL	Trent	WM03BXP	First	Y308HUA	National Express	YN04GKX	National Express
V215EGV	Galloway	WM04NYV	First	Y309HUA	National Express	YN04GKY	National Express
V345EKW	Yorkshire Trac	WM04NYW	First	Y311HUA	National Express	YN04GLF	National Express
V447EAL	Dunn-Line	WM04NZU	First	Y312HUA	National Express	YN04GLJ	National Express
V448EAL	Dunn-Line	WM04PHK	First	Y313HUA	National Express	YN04GPF	National Express
V449EAL	Dunn-Line	WV02EUP	First	Y314HUA	National Express	YN04GPJ	National Express
V839JAT	East Yorkshire	WV02EUR	First	Y315HUA	National Express	YN04GPK	National Express
V840JAT	East Yorkshire	WV02EUT	First	Y317HUA	National Express	YN04GPU	National Express
V841JAT	East Yorkshire	WV02EUU	First	Y319HUA	National Express	YN04GPV	National Express
V842JAT	East Yorkshire	WV52AKY	First	Y322HUA	National Express	YN04GPX	National Express
V843JAT	East Yorkshire	WV52FAM	First	Y324HUA	National Express	YN04YHW	First
V904DPN	Stagecoach	WV52FAO	First	Y326HUA	National Express	YN04YHX	First
V905DPN	Stagecoach	WV52FCX	First	Y327HUA	National Express	YN04YHY	First
V906DPN	Stagecoach	WV52HSX	First	Y329HUA	National Express	YN04YHZ	First
V907DDY	Stagecoach	WV52HTT	First	Y331HUA	National Express	YN51XMH	Trathens
V908DDY	Stagecoach	WV52HVE	First	Y445XAT	East Yorkshire	YN51XMJ	Trathens
V909DDY	Stagecoach	WV52HVF	First	Y467HUA	Selwyns	YN51XMK	Trathens
V944VST	Rapsons	WV52KTJ	First	Y468HUA	Selwyns	YN51XML	Trathens
VU03VVW	Stagecoach	WV52KTK	First	Y469HUA	Selwyns	YN51XMU	Trathens
VU03VVX	Stagecoach	WV52KTL	First	Y475HUA	Selwyns	YN51XMV	Trathens
VU03VVY	Stagecoach	WV53FAM	First	Y476HUA	Selwyns	YN51XMW	Trathens
VU03VVZ	Stagecoach	WX03ZFG	First	Y781MFT	Go North East	YN51XMX	Trathens
VU03VWA	Stagecoach	WX51AJU	First	Y782MFT	Go North East	YN51XMZ	Trathens
VU03VWB	Stagecoach	WX51AJV	First	Y783MFT	Go North East	YN51XNC	Trathens
W30DTS	Birmingham CC	WX51AJY	First	Y784MFT	Go North East	YN51XND	Trathens
W226CDN	Selwyns	WX51AKY	First	Y785MFT	Go North East	YN51XNE	Trathens
W336CDN	National Express	WX53PFG	First	Y808MFT	Go North East	YN52VBG	Loonat
W337CDN	National Express	WX53PFJ	First	Y823HHE	National Express	YP02AAV	Birmingham CC
W338CDN	National Express	WX53WEW	First	Y824HHE	National Express	YP02AAX	Birmingham CC
W339CDN	National Express	WX53WFA	First	Y825HHE	National Express	YP52CTV	Yeomans
W381PRC	Dunn Line	WX53WFP	First	Y967PHL	Yorkshire Traction	YP52KRZ	Birmingham CC
W381UEL	Bournemouth	WX53WGF	First	YHE91	Yorkshire Traction	YR52VEO	Yeomans
W382PRC	Dunn Line	WX53WGG	First	YJ03PFX	Arriva Midlands	YR52VFA	Dunn Line
W382UEL	Bournemouth	WX53WGJ	First	YJ03PGX	Birmingham CC	YR52VFB	Dunn Line
W383PRC	Dunn Line	X20NAT	Bruces	YJ03PGY	Birmingham CC	YR52VFC	Dunn Line
W383UEL	Bournemouth	X143WNL	Arriva North East	YJ03PGZ	Birmingham CC	YS02YXR	Yorkshire Trac
W384PRC	Dunn Line	X144WNL	Arriva North East	YJ03PKK	Birmingham CC	YS02YXT	Yorkshire Trac
W384UEL	Bournemouth	X191HFB	First	YJ03PNN	Birmingham CC	YS02YYF	Loonat
W385PRC	Dunn Line	X192HFB	First	YJ03PPY	Selwyns	YSU874	Go North East
W386PRC	Dunn Line	X193HFB	First	YJ03PPZ	Selwyns	YSU875	Go North East
W387PRC	Dunn Line	X194HFB	First	YJ04BKF	Arriva Midlands	YSU876	Go North East
W388PRC	Dunn Line	X421WVO	Birmingham CC	YJ04BYH	Selwyns	YTC49	Yorkshire Traction
W389PPC	Dunn Line	X422WVO	Birmingham CC	YJ04BYK	Selwyns	YTC856	Yorkshire Traction
W431RBB	Birmingham CC	X423WVO	Birmingham CC	YJ51EKX	Selwyns	YU04YAG	Yorkshire Trac
W432RBB	Birmingham CC	X465SAS	Rapsons	YJ51EKY	Selwyns	YU04YAH	Yorkshire Trac
W634MKY	Yeomans	X913ERA	Trent	YJ51EKZ	Selwyns	YU04YBF	Yorkshire Trac
W844SKH	East Yorkshire	X914ERA	Trent	YJ53VDN	Selwyns	YU04YBG	Yorkshire Trac
W922PCD	National Express	X915ERA	Trent	YJ53VDO	Selwyns	YV03TZN	Stagecoach
W923PCD	National Express	XIJ602	Rapsons	YJ53VFY	Arriva Midlands	YX02JFY	East Yorkshire
W924PCD	National Express	Y93HTX	Bebb	YJ53VHF	Birmingham CC		
W926PCD	National Express	Y94HTX	Bebb	YN03DFZ	Dunn Line		
WK02UMA	First	Y96HTX	Bebb	YN03DGE	Dunn Line		

ISBN 1 904875 04 1

© Published by *British Bus Publishing Ltd, September 2004*
British Bus Publishing Ltd, 16 St Margaret's Drive, Telford, TF1 3PH
httm//www.britishbuspublishing.co.uk - Telephone: 01952 255669 - Facsimile: 01952 222397